16 Extraordinary

Hispanic Americans

Nancy Lobb

J. Weston
WALCH
PUBLISHER
Portland, Maine

Photo Credits

Cesar Chavez   © 1995 AP/WIDE WORLD PHOTOS

Joan Baez   © 1987 AP/WIDE WORLD PHOTOS

Ellen Ochoa   Photo courtesy of NASA

Jaime Escalante   © 1995 AP/WIDE WORLD PHOTOS

Edward James Olmos   © 1986 UPI/BETTMANN

Judy Baca   Photo courtesy of Social and Public Art Resource Center

Sandra Cisneros   © 1995 AP/WIDE WORLD PHOTOS

Roberto Clemente   © 1995 AP/WIDE WORLD PHOTOS

Antonia Hernandez   Photo courtesy of Mexican American Legal Defense and Educational Fund

Lupe Anguiano   Photo courtesy of Institute of Texan Culture

Henry B. Gonzalez   © 1995 AP/WIDE WORLD PHOTOS

Roberto Goizueta   © 1995 REUTERS/BETTMANN

Rita Moreno   © 1995 AP/WIDE WORLD PHOTOS

Antonia Novello   © 1990 REUTERS/BETTMANN

José Feliciano   © 1995 UPI/BETTMANN

Ileana Ros-Lehtinen   © 1995 AP/WIDE WORLD PHOTOS

1 2 3 4 5 6 7 8 9 10

ISBN 0-8251-2825-0

Copyright © 1995
J. Weston Walch, Publisher
P.O. Box 658 • Portland, Maine 04104-0658

Printed in the United States of America

Contents

Introduction

The lives of many Hispanic Americans have made a difference in the story of America. Writers, artists, scientists, teachers, politicians, ministers, lawyers, doctors, businesspeople, athletes, and so many more have helped to make America what it is today. Hispanic Americans can be proud of their heritage. And it is a pride all Americans should share.

In this book you will read the stories of:

- Cesar Chavez, who used nonviolent tactics to gain better wages and working conditions for farmworkers

- Joan Baez, the internationally famous folk singer who has worked for antiwar and civil rights causes

- Ellen Ochoa, an astronaut who soared into outer space on the space shuttle *Discovery*

- Jaime Escalante, whose tough teaching methods and belief in his students inspired them to excel in mathematics

- Edward James Olmos, an award-winning actor who speaks out against violence and promotes education

- Judy Baca, an artist who planned and helped young people paint the largest outdoor mural in the world

- Sandra Cisneros, a major writer who tells the stories of strong Hispanic women

- Roberto Clemente, the first Hispanic American to enter the Baseball Hall of Fame

- Antonia Hernandez, who is president of the Mexican-American Legal Defense Fund and has worked hard for minority rights

- Lupe Anguiano, a former nun who has worked to improve education for Mexican Americans and to help women get off welfare

- Henry B. Gonzalez, who has served the American people with honesty and independence since being elected to Congress in 1961

- Roberto Goizueta, who, as chairman of the Coca-Cola Company, is in the top ranks of American business

- Rita Moreno, the only performer who has won an Oscar, a Grammy award, and two Emmy awards

- Antonia Novello, the first woman and the first Hispanic American to serve as surgeon general of the United States

- José Feliciano, who, despite blindness and poverty, became an internationally known singer and guitarist

- Ileana Ros-Lehtinen, the first Hispanic-American woman to be elected to the United States Congress

Who are the Hispanic Americans?

They are Americans whose families can be traced back to Spanish-speaking countries. The three largest groups are Mexican Americans, Puerto Ricans, and Cuban Americans. Hispanic Americans may also come from Spain, Portugal, and Central or South America.

Some people of Hispanic origin prefer to be called *Latino*. Others call themselves Mexican American, Cuban American, Puerto Ricans, etc. Some people with Mexican ties like the term *Chicano*. In this book we use the term Hispanic American to refer to all Americans with Spanish-speaking ancestors.

How many Americans are Hispanic?

There were 22,400,000 Hispanic Americans in the United States at the time of the 1990 census.

Where do Hispanic Americans live?

Most Mexican Americans live in Texas, New Mexico, Colorado, Arizona, and California. Puerto Ricans live mostly in New York, New Jersey, and Illinois. Most Cubans live in Florida.

Why are so many countries Spanish-speaking?

Spain was once a world power. In the 1400's and 1500's the Spanish explored many new parts of the world. They settled much of North and South America. Today, most of Central and South America is Spanish-speaking.

Why did Hispanics come to the United States?

MEXICANS

Mexico lost a good deal of land to the United States when it lost the Mexican War in 1848. Most of the Mexican people who lived on this land became U.S. citizens.

More recently, many Mexicans have come to the U.S. looking for work.

CUBANS

Before 1959 there were few Cuban immigrants. In 1959 Fidel Castro took over Cuba and declared it a communist country. He outlawed the owning of property. Many middle- and upper-class Cubans fled to Miami.

A second large group of Cubans came to the United States in 1980. Many of these "boat-lift" people were of lower class. Some were criminals or other people Castro wanted to get rid of.

PUERTO RICANS

Puerto Rico became a possession of the United States in 1898. In 1911 Puerto Ricans were granted U.S. citizenship. Since then, they have had the right to travel between the island and the U.S. mainland as they wish.

OTHER COUNTRIES

Other immigrants come to the United States from Nicaragua, Guatemala, Honduras, Colombia, the Dominican Republic, and El Salvador. Most come to escape civil war and political repression.

The motto on the Great Seal of the United States reads *E Pluribus Unum*. That is Latin for "Out of Many, One." The United States is made up of many peoples of many races. These peoples have come together to form one nation. Each group has been an important part of American history. I hope you will enjoy reading about sixteen Hispanic Americans who have made a difference.

—Nancy Lobb

Cesar Chavez: Civil Rights Champion

Cesar Chavez

A saint. A hero. The Mexican-American Dr. Martin Luther King, Jr. All these things have been said about Cesar Chavez.

Chavez was a civil rights leader. He led *La Causa*, the farmworkers' fight for their rights. Chavez won great gains for farmworkers.

Cesar Chavez was born in 1927 near Yuma, Arizona. In 1938 his family could not pay their taxes. So, they lost their farm. With many others, they left for California, where they had heard there was work.

The Chavez family became migrant workers. They traveled from farm to farm, picking crops. They lived in labor camps. Home might be a tent, or it might be a one-room shack. For sure there would be no running water and no bathroom.

1

The life of the migrant workers was hard. Most of the work was "stoop labor." That meant the pickers had to bend over all day to pick the crops. They were paid very little.

Some farmers even cheated the workers out of the little they earned. The workers could not speak English. So there was little they could do to fight back. They also feared being sent back to Mexico. Life there was even harder.

The Chavez children went to school when they could. Chavez later said he went to over sixty-five grade schools "for a day, a week or a few months." Chavez finished eighth grade. This was far more education than most migrant children got.

But Chavez also taught himself. He was always reading. He loved the works of Mahatma Gandhi and Dr. Martin Luther King, Jr. From these men he learned the idea of nonviolent protest.

During World War II, Chavez served in the Navy. When he returned, he married his girlfriend, Helen. They began working on a farm near San Jose with seven other family members. Later Chavez figured out that the nine workers put together were making twenty-three cents an hour!

Chavez joined the Community Service Organization (CSO). This group was working to help Mexican Americans better themselves.

Chavez worked in the fields by day. At night he worked to get Mexican Americans to register to vote. In just two months he signed up 4,000 workers.

The farm owners found out what Chavez was doing. They were afraid he would make trouble. So they fired him. Chavez began working full time for the CSO. He held meetings to talk with workers. More workers joined the CSO.

Chavez worked ten years for the CSO. Then in 1962 he left the group. Chavez wanted to form a farmworkers union. The CSO did not. So Chavez went out on his own.

Chavez, his wife, and eight children moved to Delano, California. Using their life savings of $1,200, they formed the National

Farm Workers Association (NFWA). This group later became the United Farm Workers (UFW).

Workers were glad to sign up. Their motto was the phrase "¡Sí, se puede!" ("Yes, it can be done!") This was the beginning of Chavez's life work.

Only three years later, the NFWA gained the world's attention. It joined a strike, or *huelga*, against grape growers in the Delano area. It was this *huelga* that brought fame to Chavez.

Strikes, fasts, and marches. With these tools, Chavez proved that farmworkers had power. Together they could bargain with farmers for better wages and working conditions.

It all began when Filipino grape pickers struck for higher wages. The NFWA joined in. The strike was to go on for five years.

The story of Chavez and the migrant workers soon reached the ears of all America. Newspapers and TV spread the story of *La Causa*. In 1966 ten thousand people from all over the United States marched on the state capital in Sacramento. Still the grape growers would not give in.

Chavez knew the public supported the farmworkers. So he announced a boycott of California grapes. This meant that no one would buy grapes unless farmers met some of the workers' demands.

Chavez sent workers to different cities all around the United States. They asked store owners not to sell grapes. They asked the public not to buy grapes. Many truck drivers agreed not to haul grapes. The boycott spread. Many grape growers went out of business. But still the strike went on.

After a few years, some of the strikers began to get tired. They wanted to use more violent methods of getting what they wanted. Riots, dynamite, and shooting were suggested. But Chavez insisted on using only nonviolent tactics. To bring attention to this point, he began a twenty-five-day hunger strike.

Chavez won the support of civil rights groups and churches. Many famous Americans joined *La Causa*. Robert Kennedy was a close friend of Chavez. Dr. Martin Luther King, Jr., supported Chavez. Union leaders and even the pope supported *La Causa*. Money to help the striking workers came too. At last, the grape growers gave in. After five years, the grape boycott was over. So was the strike. Chavez and the farmworkers had won.

Over the next twenty years, *La Causa* went on. Chavez kept working to help the farmworkers. He demanded an end to the use of dangerous pesticides on crops. He won rest periods for pickers. And the hated short hoe was banned.

In the 1970's Chavez led a lettuce boycott and another grape boycott. In a 1972 protest over right-to-work laws he went on a twenty-four-day fast. In 1988 he went on a thirty-six-day fast to protest the use of pesticides in fields. This fast caused much damage to his kidneys.

In 1993 Chavez died at the age of sixty-six. Doctors said his death was caused by fasting and his life of hardship.

Cesar Chavez had devoted his life to *La Causa*. All his life he chose to live penniless. He never owned a house or a car. He never took enough money to live on, earning only $6,000 his last year. The rest of the money he raised he poured back into the UFW. Although his health was failing in his later years, he never quit working for the union.

Cesar Chavez was one of the truly heroic figures of the twentieth century. He gave dignity and hope not only to farmworkers, but to all Mexican Americans. Cesar Chavez was a giant in the civil rights movement of the United States.

Remembering the Facts

1. Why did the Chavez family lose their farm?

2. What is "stoop labor"?

3. Why didn't the migrant workers fight back when they were poorly treated by large growers?

4. How did Chavez educate himself?

5. What was the purpose of the Community Service Organization?

6. Where did Chavez get the money to form the National Farm Workers Association?

7. How long was the 1965 strike against the grape growers?

8. What were some of the nonviolent tactics used by Chavez?

Understanding the Story

9.   Cesar Chavez used only nonviolent protest. If he had allowed his union members to use violence, what do you think might have happened?

10.   Cesar Chavez was fighting for the farmworkers at the same time Dr. Martin Luther King, Jr., was fighting for civil rights for African Americans. In what ways are their lives alike?

11.   Why do you think Cesar Chavez chose to live his life penniless?

Getting the Main Idea

Why do you think Cesar Chavez is a good role model for the youth of today?

Applying What You've Learned

Imagine that you are a Mexican-American teenager living in California in the 1950's. Your family all work as migrant farmworkers. Describe a day in your life.

Joan Baez:
Singer and Activist

Joan Baez was born in New York in 1941. Her father taught physics. His family had come to the United States from Mexico when he was two years old. Baez's mother was from Scotland.

Joan Baez

The Baez family were Quakers. The Quaker religion teaches nonviolence. This idea would become the guiding force of Joan's life and her music.

As a child, Baez struggled in school. She was absent as much as she attended. Many years later she learned that she was dyslexic. This made reading and other school subjects hard for her.

But Baez was talented in art and music. In high school she began singing and playing the guitar for groups of friends. Soon she was asked to play for groups around her area.

The Baez family moved to Boston. Boston had many coffee-houses and clubs where folk music was popular. Soon Joan was a part of the folk music scene.

Folk songs fit the mood of the young people of America in the 1950's and early 1960's. It was a time of protest. The civil rights movement was growing. Joan Baez became the best known of the folk singers.

In 1959 Baez made her professional debut. The eighteen-year-old amazed thirteen thousand people at the Newport Jazz Festival. Her hair was long and straight. She was barefoot. And she leaped to instant stardom.

Several record companies wanted her. She signed a contract with Vanguard, a small folk music label. Her first record album, *Joan Baez*, came out in 1960.

In 1962 *Time* magazine did a cover story on Baez. The story said that "her voice is as clear as air in the autumn, a vibrant, strong, untrained and thrilling soprano." It went on to dub Joan Baez the Queen of Folk Music.

Baez sang songs that were very, very old. But she was in tune with the problems of her day. In 1962 she became involved in the civil rights movement. On tour in the South, she performed only at black colleges. She did this to protest discrimination against blacks at other colleges. She took part in marches with Dr. Martin Luther King, Jr.

Soon Baez began singing more modern songs. In 1963 she met Bob Dylan, a powerful writer of protest songs. Dylan and Baez began to do concerts together. They became known as the King and Queen of Folk Music.

True to her Quaker roots, Baez has always stood for nonviolence. From 1964 on, she withheld the part of her income taxes which she figured would have been spent on war and weapons. She went to jail twice for her anti-Vietnam War protests. Baez's version of the song "We Shall Overcome" became the anthem of the civil rights and antiwar movements.

She was involved in other causes too. She supported Cesar Chavez and *La Causa*. Years later, she sang at the Farm Aid Concert.

By 1965 folk music was being replaced by a rock music trend led by the Beatles. Bob Dylan broke away from the folk sound and from Baez.

After 1965 Baez's musical career went in different directions. She recorded several albums in Nashville, home of country music. She also recorded a number of rock ballads.

In 1968 Baez married David Harris. Harris was later jailed for three years for refusing to be drafted. They had one son. The marriage lasted only three years.

In the 1970's Baez began to sing more about her personal life and feelings. But her support of causes never stopped. It would be impossible to list every cause she has supported.

Baez is involved with Latin American issues. In 1974 she did an album in Spanish. She has toured in Latin America. People there see her as their spokesperson.

In 1979 Baez founded the Humanitas International Human Rights Committee. The purpose of this group is to address human rights issues. It is also concerned with nonviolence and ending war.

In fact, in the 1970's Baez spent more time on activism than on her music. She became a one-woman human rights committee.

Baez has performed at countless benefit concerts. In 1985 she performed at the Live Aid Concert to fight world hunger. In 1986 she sang for Amnesty International's Conspiracy of Hope tour. In 1988 she sang for a benefit for Amnesty International.

By the 1980's Baez was seen by many as "old-fashioned" in the world of rock music. However, in the 1990's Baez decided to make a comeback. She was ready to devote more time to her music.

Her 1992 album *Play Me Backwards* was proclaimed one of the best Baez albums in years. Many critics said that Baez was sounding better than ever.

In 1993 Baez was asked to perform in the war-torn cities of Sarajevo and Zagreb in the former Yugoslavia. Although she was in the middle of a tour at the time, she canceled performances and went to Sarajevo. She said, "In a situation like this (wartime), the only thing that gives people any hope, any beauty, anything to refresh the soul is the arts."

Indeed, Baez's art is a testament to the power of music. Her songs have healed and inspired generations of Americans.

Baez has received many awards in her career—some for music, some for her human rights work. As of 1994 she has done thirty albums. Eight of these became gold records. She has also been awarded two honorary doctorate degrees.

In Baez's long career she has been an outstanding example of combining social activism with a musical career. She has a strong belief in nonviolence. All her life she has acted on these beliefs, both in her music and in her dedication to her causes.

Remembering the Facts

1. What teaching of the Quaker religion became the guiding principle of Joan Baez's life?

2. Why did Joan Baez do poorly in school?

3. In what two areas was Baez talented?

    a.   b.

4. In what type of music did Baez get her start?

5. When and where did Baez gain instant stardom?

6. Name two causes supported by Baez in the 1960's.

    a.

    b.

7. Why did Baez do less with her music in the 1970's and 1980's?

8. Why did Baez decide to make a comeback in the 1990's?

Understanding the Story

9. Music can be a powerful way to influence the thinking of others. How do you think Joan Baez used her music to influence the youth of America in a positive way?

10. Joan Baez did a concert in Sarajevo in 1993. At that time, the city had been under siege for a year. As she sang, the audience could hear shelling in the background. After the concert, one person told her, "Thank you for coming here. You've brought us life." Why do you think the person said that?

Getting the Main Idea

Why do you think Joan Baez is a good role model for the youth of today?

Applying What You've Learned

Imagine that you are a songwriter. You want to share with others of your age an idea that is important to you. Write a song or poem that explains your idea.

Ellen Ochoa:
Astronaut

September 12, 1993. It was a beautiful day at Cape Canaveral, Florida. The space shuttle *Discovery*'s engines roared to life. Its mission in space was about to begin.

On board *Discovery* were five astronauts. One of them was Dr. Ellen Ochoa. She was the first female Hispanic astronaut.

Ochoa was born in 1958 in Los Angeles, California. She grew up in La Mesa, California, with three brothers and a sister.

Ochoa's father worked for Sears. Her mother stayed home to raise their five children.

Ellen Ochoa

When Ochoa was in middle school, her parents were divorced. Ochoa credits her mother with her success.

Ochoa's mother told her children they could succeed at whatever they wanted to do. She stressed the value of a college education. All the Ochoa children worked hard and did well in school.

Ellen Ochoa was a good student. She loved math and science. But she did well in all her courses.

When she was thirteen, Ochoa won the San Diego County spelling bee. She graduated from high school first in her class.

Ochoa won a scholarship to Stanford. But she turned it down. She needed to stay closer to home. Her mother needed help with Ellen's younger brothers.

So Ochoa went to San Diego State University instead. There she earned a degree in physics. Again she graduated first in her class.

Ochoa went on to Stanford. There she earned a Ph.D. in electrical engineering. During all her years in school, she earned straight A's. She was not only a hard worker, but also a brilliant student.

But Ochoa had no thought of becoming an astronaut while she was in school. In fact, she couldn't decide what to study in college. She changed her major five times at San Diego State. First music, then business, journalism, and computer science tempted her. Finally, she settled on physics.

Ochoa always had a lot of interests. In high school, she became an excellent flutist. She won several awards for her playing. And she nearly chose flute-playing as a career. She decided she couldn't make enough money that way. But she still plays the flute as a hobby.

Another of Ochoa's hobbies has been flying. In 1988 she got her pilot's license for small planes. At that point she had become interested in being an astronaut. So, she thought she should learn more about flying.

From 1985 to 1988 Ochoa worked as a researcher. During this time she received three patents in optical processing.

Ochoa first applied to become an astronaut in 1985. But she was turned down. She didn't give up. She applied again in 1987. This time she was accepted as one of one hundred finalists.

In 1988 she began working for NASA. She began as a researcher. But she moved up the ladder quickly. Soon she was supervising thirty-five other scientists.

In 1990 Ochoa married Coe Miles. Miles is also a research engineer.

Ochoa graduated in the astronaut class of 1990. She became a missions specialist.

Ochoa spent the next three years preparing to go on her first space flight. There was a lot to learn.

She would be going aboard the *Discovery* space shuttle. In the *Discovery*'s cargo bay is a science laboratory. It is called ATLAS-2. Ochoa would be one of two scientists working there.

The purpose of the mission was to study the earth's atmosphere. Ochoa would study the ozone layer. This is the part of the atmosphere that protects the earth from the sun's harmful ultraviolet rays. In recent years, the ozone layer has thinned. Ochoa hoped to learn more about this problem.

Getting her chance to soar in outer space took some patience. The shuttle was first scheduled to take off in March 1993. It had to be rescheduled for April 7. That takeoff had to be scrapped too.

Next, the mission was set for August 12. Everything seemed to be going smoothly. The countdown got to three seconds from lift-off. But there was trouble on the launchpad. Again, the mission was halted.

"Try, try, again . . ." The ten-day mission was rescheduled for September 12, 1993. At last, everything fell into place. *Discovery* took off, and Ellen Ochoa had become the first Hispanic woman to fly into outer space.

During the flight, Ochoa and the other astronauts deployed instruments that would allow scientists to gather more information about the changes taking place in the ozone layer.

On November 3, 1994, Ochoa went on her second mission. Space shuttle *Atlantis* did the most in-depth study yet of the earth's atmosphere and its ozone layer.

When Ochoa became an astronaut, she decided that she wanted to be a good role model for young people. She knows that being an astronaut puts her in a position where students will listen to her. Ochoa tries to show them that study and hard work can pay off in a good job.

Ochoa spends a lot of time speaking at schools. She encourages young people, especially girls, to study math and science. She hopes that her success will show that anyone who works hard enough in school and on the job can succeed.

Ochoa works hard. But she takes time to enjoy the beauty of life too. On the shuttle Ochoa took along her flute. That way she could relax with some out-of-this-world music.

Remembering the Facts

1. For what "first" is Ellen Ochoa famous?

2. Where was Ochoa born?

3. Why does Ochoa credit her mother for her own success?

4. Why did Ochoa turn down a scholarship to Stanford?

5. What musical instrument does Ochoa play?

6. Why did Ochoa get her pilot's license?

7. In what field does Ochoa hold three patents?

8. What was the purpose of the ATLAS-2 mission?

9. Why is the ozone layer of the atmosphere important?

10. What is the message Ellen Ochoa brings when she speaks to children in schools?

Understanding the Story

11. Ellen Ochoa's mother took college courses for twenty-three years before graduating with a triple major. Why do you think she was such a strong influence on Ellen?

12. Why do you think Ochoa enjoys speaking at schools, especially to young girls?

Getting the Main Idea

Why is Ellen Ochoa a good role model for the youth of today?

Applying What You've Learned

Write a series of headlines to show the sequence of achievements in Ellen Ochoa's life—for example:

Spellin' Is for Ellen!
Ellen Ochoa Wins Spelling Bee

Jaime Escalante: Math Teacher

Jaime Escalante was born in 1930 in Bolivia. His parents were both teachers. They taught in a small Indian village.

Family life for Escalante was not happy. His father drank too much and beat his wife. When Escalante was nine years old, his mother left his father. She moved her five children to La Paz, Bolivia.

When Escalante was fourteen, his mother sent him to a private high school. In school Escalante was known for his jokes. He was also a good fighter. He usually tried to get out of doing his homework. But he couldn't get enough of math and science.

Escalante finished high school. He decided to train to become a teacher.

Jaime Escalante

When Escalante was in his second year of college, a local high school physics teacher died. Escalante was asked to take his place. At the same time, he kept studying to complete his teaching degree.

In 1954 Escalante got a job teaching physics at his old high school. At the same time, he taught part-time at two other schools.

Escalante was a tough teacher. He assigned his students fifty to a hundred problems a night. A student who broke the rules might get another two hundred problems. He pushed all his students to their limit. His motto was, "What is mediocre is useless."

Escalante soon became known as a great teacher. His students won many awards. But teachers were not well paid. Escalante had to work at three or four jobs. He decided to move his family to Los Angeles.

But Escalante was in for a shock. To teach in the United States, he would have to repeat college. California would not accept his Bolivian teaching degree. That meant four years of college and one year of graduate study before he could teach.

He began taking night courses at Pasadena City College. To support his family, he took a job washing floors in a restaurant. Soon, he became its chief cook.

Escalante was a good student. But it was slow going to school part-time. Then Escalante won a scholarship. Now he could go to school full-time. He got his teaching degree at the age of forty-three.

Escalante started to teach math at Garfield High School. This school was in the barrio of East Los Angeles. Its students came from poor families. The school was overrun with gangs. Graffiti covered the walls. Trash was all over the school grounds. Most of the students did not finish high school.

Escalante went to work. On Saturdays he came to school and cleaned up his room. He and some students painted. He put up posters of the L.A. Lakers.

And he set to work on his students. He pushed them hard. He decided that the math book was far too easy. He asked the principal for new books. He was told there was no money. After he threatened to quit, money was found.

Escalante looked past the background of his students. He saw many of them had a lot of ability. He began teaching harder math courses. Finally, he added a course in calculus.

In his first year of teaching calculus, only five students passed the course. Everyone else dropped out.

The story that made Escalante famous involved the Advanced Placement exam for calculus. The Advanced Placement exam is a national test given at the end of the school year. Students across the country who pass the test are given college credit for the course. The test is hard. Very few students in the country pass. But the first year Escalante taught calculus, two of his five students passed.

That was good. But Escalante knew he could do better. He scouted the lower grades for good students. Each year his calculus courses were a little larger. And more of his students passed the Advanced Placement exam for calculus.

In 1982 eighteen Garfield High students took the AP Calculus exam. *All* of the students passed. This kind of success was unheard of.

But then the test correctors noted a problem. Twelve of the students had solved one of the problems in the same way. They accused the students of cheating on the exam. The scores were thrown out.

Escalante and his principal complained. Some of the students' parents complained too.

Finally the testers agreed that the students could retake the test. So in August all the students took the test again. But it had been months since the last test. Would they remember their calculus well enough to pass?

They did! Again all the students passed. All won college credit for calculus. They had not cheated. They had solved the problems in the same way because that was how they had been taught.

The story hit the newspapers across the country. No one could believe that a school like Garfield could have so many students pass the AP test. Most schools, even in wealthy areas, only had a few pass each year. Yet Garfield, in the barrio of East Los Angeles, had eighteen.

The reason was Jaime Escalante. He believed in his students. He kindly yet firmly insisted that they do the tough work he assigned. Anyone who did not work hard could expect a call to their parents. And extra work before school, after school and/or on weekends.

Escalante's classroom became a showcase. Visiting teachers and principals studied his teaching methods.

The story of Escalante's life was shown in the hit movie *Stand and Deliver*. Escalante was played by Edward James Olmos. The movie made Escalante the most famous math teacher in America.

Escalante himself stars in a PBS series called *Futures*. The series shows how math is important for success on the job. He has also done a PBS show with Bill Cosby called *Math . . . Who Needs It?*

Today, Escalante's new students know what to expect. One thing is for sure: They will work hard, and they will succeed. And they will always remember Escalante's rule:

"Determination + Hard Work + Discipline = The Way to Success."

Remembering the Facts

1. In what country was Escalante born?

2. What two subjects were Escalante's favorites in school?

    a.   b.

3. Why did Escalante decide to move to the United States?

4. What did Escalante have to do before he could teach in the United States?

5. Name three problems Escalante faced when he started teaching at Garfield High.

    a.

    b.

    c.

6. What is the purpose of taking an AP test?

7. Why did the test correctors think Escalante's students had cheated on the AP test?

8. Name the movie that tells Escalante's life story.

9. What three things make up Escalante's winning formula for success?

    a.

    b.

    c.

Understanding the Story

10. Escalante has had great success teaching math to students from poor backgrounds. Do you think other teachers could use his methods and have the same success? Why or why not?

11. Explain Escalante's motto: "What is mediocre is useless."

Getting the Main Idea

Why do you think Jaime Escalante is a good role model for the youth of today?

Applying What You've Learned

Imagine you are writing the script for an episode of *Futures*. Choose a job that interests you. Choose a famous guest to co-host your show with you. Make a list of ways you and your co-host could show how math is used in the job you've chosen for your episode.

Edward James Olmos:
Activist Actor

Edward James Olmos has been called the best Hispanic-American actor of today. Make that one of the best actors of today! Olmos is a hero to many Hispanic Americans. He is proof that with hard work people can become whatever they want.

Olmos was born in East Los Angeles in 1947. His father was an immigrant from Mexico. His mother was a Mexican American.

When Olmos was very young, his parents divorced. The three Olmos children were raised by their mother in a small house in East Los Angeles. It was a diverse neighborhood. Hispanics, Native Americans, and various immigrants lived together. All were poor.

Edward James Olmos

Olmos wanted to escape his poverty. He knew he must stay out of street gangs. He knew he must stay off drugs.

He decided his way out would be baseball. He worked hard to improve. And he did. He won the Golden State batting championship.

25

But at the age of fifteen, Olmos lost interest in baseball. He decided he wanted to be a singer. So, he took singing lessons. He taught himself to play the piano. He started a band called Eddie James and the Pacific Ocean. Olmos was the lead singer.

Soon the band had a nightly job at a club on Sunset Strip. During the day, Olmos went to East Los Angeles City College.

Olmos feared public speaking. So he signed up for a drama class. He liked it so much, he dropped his idea of being a singer. He decided to be an actor.

Success in acting did not come right away. So he worked as a mover to support his wife and young family. Soon he landed some bit parts in TV shows and movies.

Olmos's first starring role was in *Zoot Suit*. This was the story of a group of Mexican-American youths wrongly convicted of a murder in Los Angeles in 1942. Olmos played the role of El Pachuco.

El Pachuco is a symbol of the proud Chicano spirit that arose in the California of the 1940's. To Olmos, the part was important because he was playing the first true-to-life Hispanic character ever seen on the American stage.

For this role, Olmos won the Los Angeles Critics Circle Award. When the play moved to Broadway, he was nominated for a Tony Award. Later, Olmos starred in the movie version of the play as well.

In the 1983 movie *The Ballad of Gregory Cortez*, Olmos had the lead role. He played a young Mexican cowboy who was hunted down by a 600-man posse led by Texas Rangers. This true story showed the prejudice against Mexicans in Texas in the early 1900's.

It was the TV series *Miami Vice* that brought fame to Olmos. For his work on the show, Olmos won an Emmy for best supporting actor in 1985. He won a Golden Globe award in 1986. He was one of the first Hispanic actors to have a leading role on a long-lasting (five years) TV show.

One of Olmos's favorite roles was that of Jaime Escalante in the movie *Stand and Deliver*. Escalante was a math teacher in the barrio of East Los Angeles. He pushed eighteen of his students into passing the Advanced Placement test in calculus.

Stand and Deliver was an important movie to the Hispanic community. It gave a message of hope to those living in poverty. It showed that belief in oneself and hard work are what it takes to succeed.

To play the part of Escalante, Olmos gained forty pounds. And he spent hundreds of hours watching Escalante teach. He learned Escalante's speech patterns and mannerisms. For his efforts, he was nominated for an Academy Award for best actor.

Another movie Olmos made was *American Me*. This movie warned about crime and violence in America. It is the story of a drug lord named Santana. While in prison, Santana creates and leads the Mexican Mafia.

This 1992 anti-gang movie angered the real Mexican Mafia. They made threats on Olmos's life. Four people who worked on the movie were subsequently killed under mysterious circumstances.

Olmos has had a fine career in acting. But he is also known as an activist. This is no public relations stunt. Olmos is deeply committed to helping the down-and-out.

Olmos spends more than half his time visiting prisons and detention centers. He speaks on Indian reservations and at hospitals. He speaks at high schools. And he is in great demand at teachers' meetings. On the average he gives one hundred fifty talks per year.

Olmos's motto is, "If they call and I'm available, I'll go." He has often made a one-day round-trip from Miami to Los Angeles to give a forty-five-minute talk.

What is Olmos's message? He is against violence and gangs. He is for education. The way to make a difference, he says, is by volunteerism. That means volunteering your time and talents to make a difference in your town. Olmos practices what he preaches.

In April 1992, riots broke out in Los Angeles. White police officers had been videotaped beating a black man, Rodney King. But a jury declared them innocent of the charges.

Angry mobs rioted. There was destruction of property all over the city. Olmos offered his help to mayor Tom Bradley right away.

Olmos seemed to be everywhere during the riots. He appeared on TV, asking for calm. He talked to those whose property was destroyed. Finally, he picked up a broom and began sweeping. Soon hundreds of people had joined him in the cleanup effort.

This is what Edward James Olmos is all about. He is a fine actor who hopes to show Hispanics in a positive light. He speaks out on issues of our day. And he has been committed to community service for the last twenty years.

Remembering the Facts

1. Where was Olmos born?

2. In what kind of neighborhood did Olmos grow up?

3. How did Olmos first hope to escape his early life of poverty?

4. Name the band Olmos started when he was fifteen.

5. Why did Olmos sign up for a drama class in college?

6. In what play did Olmos have the role of El Pachuco?

7. What TV series made Olmos famous?

8. For which movie did Olmos receive an Academy Award nomination?

9. Which anti-gang movie angered the Mexican Mafia, causing them to threaten Olmos's life?

10. Olmos is well-known as an activist. Name two causes he speaks out on.

    a.   b.

Understanding the Story

11. Olmos is in demand as a speaker. He is often scheduled two years in advance. Why do you think his message is in such demand?

12. Olmos has a dream of turning his great-grandparents' house in the barrio of East Los Angeles into a museum. He hopes to show kids that starting from poverty they can go anywhere they want. What characteristics do you think a person would need to escape from poverty?

Getting the Main Idea

Why do you think Edward James Olmos is a good role model for the youth of today?

Applying What You've Learned

Imagine that you are on the scene of the Los Angeles riots in 1992. You are asked to give a message on TV to calm the people. What could you say to help stop the riots?

Judy Baca:
Artist

Judy Baca

The Tujunga Wash is a flood control channel of the Los Angeles River. In 1976 the Army Corps of Engineers had an unusual request. They wanted Judy Baca, a Mexican-American artist, to paint a mural on the walls.

The result was one of the most amazing urban art projects in the United States. Baca called it the *Great Wall of Los Angeles.*

The *Great Wall* is the largest outdoor mural in the world. It tells the history of California. It starts in the days of the cave dwellers. It goes all the way to the 1950's.

Judith Francisca Baca was born in 1946 in Los Angeles. She lived with her grandmother, mother, and two aunts. The family spoke Spanish at home.

The mother worked in a tire factory. So Baca was raised mostly by her grandmother. Baca did not know her father, who was a musician.

School was hard for Baca. She spoke English poorly. So, the teacher let her paint while the other children did their work. This was when Baca's love of painting began.

Baca graduated from high school in 1964. The next year she married. In 1969 she graduated from California State University in Northridge. Her degree was in art.

Her marriage ended. Baca returned to teach at her old high school. But she did not keep her job at the school for very long.

At that time, many young people were protesting the war in Vietnam. They felt we should not be sending our soldiers to fight in a civil war so far away.

Baca joined the peace movement. She took part in marches against the war. Other teachers at the school also joined in the movement.

Finally, the head of the high school fired all the teachers who took part in antiwar activities. Baca was one of them. She was very upset. She thought that no one would hire her to teach again.

Losing her teaching job forced Baca to look for another kind of job. She found a job with the City of Los Angeles Cultural Affairs Division.

In her new job, Baca taught art in the city parks. She spent a lot of time with teenagers. She soon learned that the art forms they liked best were tattoos and graffiti.

Baca started a club called Las Vistas Nuevas. The kids in the group came from four rival gangs.

Baca got the kids to paint a mural in Hollenbeck Park. The kids learned to get along. They gave up the gangs. For Baca, it was the first of many murals she would do with groups of kids.

Baca wanted to learn more about mural painting. She went to Mexico to study with famous mural painters there.

Murals are an old Mexican art form. This "art for the people" or "public art" is not kept in museums. Instead, these large paintings are done on the walls of buildings, on bridges, or on other large surfaces.

Baca returned to Los Angeles. She began the Citywide Mural Project. She brought kids of all races together to work on the project. More than two hundred fifty murals came out of this effort.

The largest of these was the *Great Wall*. This mural is actually a half-mile long. The mural tells about the history of California. It shows the many contributions made by ethnic minorities.

If you walk along the mural, you will see many things. Prehistoric animals roam a California tar pit. Spanish explorer Juan Cabrillo arrives by ship. Mexicans and Yankees fight over gold.

Chinese workers build the railroad. Migrant workers work in the fields. Hungry people line up for food during the Depression.

Japanese Americans are imprisoned during World War II. The freedom riders work for civil rights. These and many more events are pictured in the *Great Wall*.

The finished *Great Wall* is an amazing sight. But just as amazing is how it was created. The painting took over five summers to finish. Hundreds of kids of all races worked on it.

Baca raised the money to do the work. She outlined what she wanted done. She hired some workers. And she asked kids to join in the work.

In 1987 Judy Baca began another large project. It was called *World Wall: A Vision of the Future Without Fear*. This mural was to be done by artists from around the world.

The *World Wall* was made so it could be taken apart and moved. It was made in pieces each ten feet high and thirty feet long. Baca painted seven of these panels with the help of teenagers.

Artists from other countries painted another seven panels. Baca asked the artists to show their idea of "the future without fear."

In 1990 the *World Wall* went on display in Finland. Next, it was seen in Russia. It has also been shown in the Smithsonian Museum in Washington, DC.

Baca hopes that the work will spread her ideas of a world of peace—a world in which the contributions of all races are valued.

Today Baca teaches art at the University of California at Irvine. She also remains active in Hispanic-American affairs. She is a well-known spokesperson for her people.

Remembering the Facts

1. What is the name of the largest outdoor mural in the United States?

2. What story is told on this mural?

3. Where was Judy Baca born?

4. Why did Baca have trouble in school as a young girl?

5. Why did Baca lose her job teaching high school art?

6. What was Las Vistas Nuevas?

7. Name three events pictured on the *Great Wall of Los Angeles*.

    a.

    b.

    c.

8. Describe how the *Great Wall* was created.

9. What other large project did Baca begin in 1987?

10. What is the purpose of Judy Baca's "public art"?

Understanding the Story

11. Judy Baca lost her first job teaching art at a high school. In what ways was her new career in public art still a kind of teaching career?

12. Judy Baca once said, "As artists, we have the power of spreading ideas." What do you think she meant by this? Give examples of how this could be true. (You could include a variety of forms of art in your examples.)

Getting the Main Idea

Why do you think Judy Baca is a good role model for young people of today?

Applying What You've Learned

Imagine you are an artist who has been asked to create a long mural for your city. The title of the mural is to be the *Great Wall of* _____ (fill in your city's name). Write titles for panels you would put in your mural. You may sketch each panel as well.

Sandra Cisneros: Author

Sandra Cisneros is a new voice in American literature. Some think she is our best Mexican-American woman writer.

Cisneros is a pioneer. She writes stories that have never been told. She is filling the void of stories about Hispanic-American women.

Cisneros hopes that her success will open the door for many other Hispanic writers.

Cisneros was born in 1954 in Chicago, Illinois. Her father was Mexican; her mother, Mexican American.

Cisneros had six brothers. She says she felt like she grew up with seven fathers telling her what to do.

Sandra Cisneros

In her early years, Sandra and her family moved many times. When her father became homesick for Mexico, they would go back to Mexico City. They always returned to Chicago, but to a different street, a different apartment, and a different school.

But all the neighborhoods they tried had one thing in common: They were poor, with vacant lots and burned-out buildings.

All this moving was hard on Cisneros. She became very shy. She had few friends.

Cisneros spent a lot of time by herself. She developed a strong love of reading. Books became her escape from her bleak world. Later, Cisneros said that her aloneness "was good for a would-be writer. It allowed . . . time to think . . . to imagine . . . to read and prepare."

Cisneros learned to hide within herself. She became an observer of other people. She watched and remembered how they looked, how they talked, and what they did.

Cisneros's parents had little education. But they stressed education to their children. Her father worked as a carpenter. But he wanted more for his children. He often told them to learn to use their heads, not their hands.

So when Cisneros wanted to go to college, her father agreed. He thought that college would be a good place for her to find a husband. Cisneros had other ideas. At Loyola University she majored in English. She wanted to become a writer.

Cisneros started by writing poems. She studied for her master's degree at the University of Iowa Writer's Workshop. Here she studied among writers from the best schools in the country.

She soon found out that she had little in common with the other students. She felt out of place, almost foreign. Later she described herself as a "yellow weed among the city's cracks." Her classmates had been bred as "hothouse flowers."

One day in class, students were telling about the houses where they had grown up. As she listened, Cisneros realized she had no such house in her memories. As they talked, Cisneros suddenly knew why she felt different from the other students. She *was* different in her race and culture. She was a Mexican woman.

At that moment, she accepted herself for who she was. She realized her voice was unique. She had found herself. She would write about things her classmates could never write about.

From this awakening, her first book was born. *The House on Mango Street* is the story of Esperanza, a young girl growing up in a poor Hispanic neighborhood in Chicago. Through her eyes, the reader sees the lives of the people living there. In the course of the book, Esperanza learns to understand both herself and her culture.

But Esperanza wants a better life for herself. By the end of the book, she has decided how she will escape her poverty: through her writing. But at the close of the book, she is reminded that leaving Mango Street does not mean leaving who she is. In fact, the story of Esperanza is the story of Cisneros herself.

With the publication of *The House on Mango Street* in 1984, Cisneros became recognized as a major new talent. Today the book is being used in schools and colleges across the country.

After finishing *The House on Mango Street*, Cisneros received a one-year National Endowment for the Arts fellowship. She moved to Texas. There, she wrote a book of poetry, *My Wicked, Wicked Ways*.

This book got great reviews. Yet Cisneros was unable to make a living from her writing. She worked at odd jobs, trying to scrape out a living. This time was the low point of her life.

Finally, she was offered a teaching job in California. Later, she was awarded another NEA fellowship. She was back on her feet.

Meanwhile, in New York City, a literary agent had read *The House on Mango Street*. She was so moved by the book that she tried to track down Cisneros. She wanted to help her publish more books.

It took nearly four years for the two women to get together. But finally it worked out. This led to the publication, in 1991, of Cisneros's third book, *Women Hollering Creek and Other Stories*.

The title story has been called one of the great short stories in American literature.

In this book, Cisneros talks about the lives of Hispanic women. All of her characters are strong women. They are women of different ages, different races, and different situations telling their stories.

Today Cisneros lives in San Antonio, Texas. She says her hobby is collecting vintage clothes. She also likes to talk with friends and sleep. She continues to write, and her fourth book, *Loose Woman*, was published in 1994.

Cisneros hopes to give something back to the Hispanic community. While she has left her childhood of poverty behind, it is still a part of her. As one of her characters in *The House on Mango Street* tells Esperanza:

> *You will always be Esperanza. You will always be Mango Street.*
> *You can't erase what you know. You can't forget who you are.*
> *You must remember to come back. For the ones who cannot leave*
> *as easily as you.*

Cisneros will never leave the Hispanic community. She is herself a symbol of the Mexican woman. And through her writing, her story is being heard at last.

Remembering the Facts

1. Where was Cisneros born and raised?

2. Why did the Cisneros family move so often?

3. Why did Cisneros develop a love for reading?

4. Why did Cisneros's shyness help her as a writer?

5. What did Cisneros's father hope she would do at college?

6. How did Cisneros come to realize that she had a unique voice as a writer?

7. What was the name of Cisneros's first book?

8. What does Cisneros talk about in this book?

9. What is the subject of *Women Hollering Creek and Other Stories*?

10. In what way does Cisneros hope to give something back to the Hispanic community where she grew up?

Understanding the Story

11. Why do you think it is important for anyone who wants to become a writer to read a lot?

12. In what ways do you think Cisneros's childhood of poverty and loneliness made her a better writer?

13. What do you think is meant by these lines from *The House on Mango Street*?

> *You will always be Esperanza. You will always be Mango Street.*
> *You can't erase what you know. You can't forget who you are.*

Getting the Main Idea

Why do you think Sandra Cisneros is a good role model for the youth of today?

Applying What You've Learned

Imagine that you are writing a story or poem about your childhood. Make a list of events, places, and people who were important in your early life—things that make up a part of who you are.

Roberto Clemente: Baseball Player

Roberto Clemente was born in 1934 in a small town near San Juan, Puerto Rico. He was the youngest of seven children. His father was the foreman of a sugar plantation.

Even before he started school, Clemente loved to play baseball. He started with softball. Later, he played in a city league. He played so much baseball he sometimes forgot to eat.

When he wasn't playing baseball, he was listening to games on the radio. Hour after hour he squeezed a hard rubber ball. He hoped to make his arm stronger. It must have worked. Clemente had one of the best arms in baseball.

Roberto Clemente

In high school Clemente played baseball. But he was also on the school track team. He was thought to be a sure bet for the 1952 Olympic track team. But baseball got in the way.

One day Clemente was playing ball at the park. He was using a torn fielder's mitt. The owner of the Santurce Crabbers (a winter league team) saw him. He was amazed at the boy's skills. On the spot he offered Clemente a job. Clemente signed a contract for $500—and a new glove.

A year later, in 1953, a scout for the Brooklyn Dodgers spotted Clemente. The scout wanted to sign Clemente that day. But Clemente's father said no. His son must finish high school first. He wanted his son to become an engineer. That was looking less likely all the time.

When Clemente finished school, nine teams wanted him. The Dodgers offered him $10,000 to sign with them. That was the largest amount ever offered a Hispanic player.

Clemente accepted the offer. Hours later, the Milwaukee Braves offered him $30,000.

Clemente didn't know what to do. He had not signed any papers with the Dodgers. But he had agreed to the first offer. He asked his parents for advice. His mother said, "If you gave the word, you keep the word." To the Clementes, honor was more important than money. So Clemente signed with the Dodgers.

Clemente began his career in the minor leagues. His first year, he played for the Dodgers farm team in Montreal, Canada.

Clemente's first year in pro ball was not a happy one. He did not speak much English. Customs and food in Canada were strange to him. And he was a black Hispanic in a mostly white country. He felt like an outsider.

Clemente soon had a health problem too. Baseball bats in the 1950's were thick and heavy. But a new lighter bat had come out. Players could hit farther with the new bat. Clemente decided to try one out. He picked up a light bat and swung hard. That was a big mistake. He wrenched his back.

Then in 1954 a drunk driver hit Clemente's car. Again his back was hurt. Many times after that he had to sit out from games. When he did play, he was often in pain.

In 1954 Clemente was drafted by the Pittsburgh Pirates. He was the number one draft choice in the country. His first year with the Pirates, the team finished last. But Clemente played well, batting .360.

Clemente felt out of place living in Pittsburgh. After games he had no place to go. So he went down and talked to the fans before they left the stadium. It was the start of a long-lasting friendship with the Pirates fans.

With Clemente's help, the Pirates got better. He was rewarded with a big increase in pay. He used much of it to buy a new home for his parents.

During the winter of 1957, Clemente was in the United States Marines. For six months he worked long hours. The work helped his weak back. When he went back to the Pirates for the 1958 season, his back was strong again.

The 1960 season was one of Clemente's best. That year the Pirates won the National League championship. It was the first time they had won in thirty-three years. The team went on to win the World Series against the New York Yankees.

With all his fame, Clemente never forgot his roots in Puerto Rico. Every year after baseball season ended, he returned home. He spent the winter working with kids who wanted to play ball.

In 1963 Clemente married a Puerto Rican woman. They built a new home near Clemente's parents in Puerto Rico. Over the years they had three sons.

Clemente's career was booming. In 1965 he won the Most Valuable Player award for the National League. He had also become the leader of the Pirates.

In 1970 the Pirates honored Clemente by holding Roberto Clemente Night. Thousands of people came to cheer for him. He was given a gift of $6,000. Few people ever knew that Clemente gave the check to the Children's Hospital in Pittsburgh that very night. In fact, he often gave large amounts to charity. But he always kept it a secret.

Again in 1971 the Pirates, led by Clemente, won the World Series. Clemente was named the outstanding player of the series.

In the spring of 1972, Clemente made his three thousandth hit. Only ten other men in the history of baseball had equaled that feat. It would be Clemente's last regular season hit of his life.

On December 22, 1972, an earthquake hit Nicaragua. Thousands were killed. The capital city of Managua was nearly destroyed.

Roberto Clemente began setting up a Puerto Rican relief effort. He began collecting food, clothes, and medical supplies.

There were rumors that planeloads of supplies were being stolen when they arrived in Nicaragua. Clemente decided to fly on the supply plane to make sure those who needed help got it.

It was New Year's Eve. Clemente canceled his party plans. He boarded the plane for Nicaragua. Shortly after takeoff, the plane exploded. It plunged into the ocean. There were no survivors. Roberto Clemente's body has never been found.

Puerto Rico had lost its greatest hero. Baseball had lost one of its top stars. Here are some of his achievements:

> Four National League batting championships
> Three thousand hits in the major leagues
> Lifetime batting average of .317
> National League's Most Valuable Player, 1966 and 1971
> Twelve Golden Glove awards for fielding excellence
> First Hispanic American to enter Baseball Hall of Fame

Roberto Clemente was a great ballplayer. But he did all he could for those in need as well. He once said, "Any time you have the chance to do something for someone else and you don't do it, you are wasting your time on this earth." That was how Clemente lived his life. And that is why he was much more than a great ballplayer. He is remembered by many as a hero.

Remembering the Facts

1. With what team did Clemente sign his first contract (for $500)?

2. Why did Clemente sign a contract with the Dodgers when the Braves offered him more money?

3. Why was Clemente unhappy in his first years of pro ball?

4. What two events caused Clemente's years of back pain?

   a.

   b.

5. What team drafted Clemente in 1954 as its number one draft choice?

6. What did Clemente do in the winter when baseball was over?

7. How many hits did Clemente make in his major league career?

8. Why did Clemente go on the plane with the medical supplies for Nicaragua?

9. Name three awards won by Clemente during his career.

    a.

    b.

    c.

Understanding the Story

10. Why do you think Roberto Clemente was a hero to many Puerto Ricans?

11. When Clemente gave gifts to charity, he always kept it a secret. What do you think that tells about the kind of man he was?

12. Most Hispanic-American ballplayers led two lives. During baseball season they lived on the mainland. During the off-season, they went home to their native country. Why do you think most of them did this, rather than stay in the United States full-time?

Getting the Main Idea

Why do you think Roberto Clemente is a good role model for the young people of today?

Applying What You've Learned

Imagine that you are in charge of organizing relief efforts for victims of an earthquake. Write a newspaper ad asking for donations of money, food, and clothing from citizens of your area.

Antonia Hernandez: Civil Rights Lawyer

The Mexican-American Legal Defense Fund (MALDEF) is a Hispanic civil rights group. Antonia Hernandez is MALDEF's president and general counsel.

MALDEF was founded in 1968. Its purpose is to protect the legal rights of Mexican Americans. MALDEF works for better education for Mexican Americans. The group also seeks job training for minorities.

Since 1985, Antonia Hernandez has led MALDEF. She has fought for the rights of Hispanics and other minority groups. "We are the Hispanic community's law firm," she says.

Antonia Hernandez

Antonia Hernandez was born in 1948 in Torreón, Mexico. When she was eight, her family moved to East Los Angeles. Her father was a gardener. Her mother stayed home to raise the six Hernandez children.

The Hernandez family was poor. But it was strong and loving. Hernandez's parents encouraged their children to do well in school. They also gave the children a strong belief in helping others.

Hernandez trained to be a teacher. She graduated from UCLA in 1973 with a teaching certificate. She began working in a ghetto program for teenagers. Soon she decided that she could help kids more by doing something about the unfair laws that were keeping them back.

So Hernandez went to law school at UCLA. After she graduated, she became a legal aid lawyer. Legal aid lawyers provide legal help for the poor. She also fought for pro-minority bills in the state legislature.

In 1977 she married Michael Stern, who was also a lawyer. The couple later had three children.

In 1978 Hernandez was offered a new job. She would work for the Senate Judiciary Committee under Senator Ted Kennedy. She turned down the job. She was happy doing legal aid work to help the poor of Los Angeles. And she didn't really want to leave her hometown.

The committee couldn't believe that she had turned down the job because she loved her legal aid work. They thought the real reason must be the salary. So they offered her more money.

Hernandez turned down the job again. But her husband finally talked her into it. He told her it was a career move that was too good to pass up.

So Hernandez moved to Washington, DC, to work for the Judiciary Committee. She advised the committee on immigration and human rights issues.

Hernandez worked for the committee for two years. But in 1980 the Democrats lost control of the Senate. That meant that the Republicans would take over the Judiciary Committee. And Antonia Hernandez was out of a job.

The next day she had a job offer from MALDEF. She joined its Washington, DC, office. She quickly worked her way up through the ranks. By 1981 she was heading the office.

While working with MALDEF, Hernandez has been able to get many laws passed to help Hispanic Americans. She has fought for fair funding for public schools. She has gone to court to make sure school district lines were drawn fairly. She has also worked for more jobs for Hispanic Americans.

And she fought against a bill that would have required Hispanics to carry I.D. cards. She said this would lead to discrimination. The defeat of this bill was one of her proudest achievements.

Hernandez has worked hard for bilingual education. "Bilingual" means being able to speak two languages equally well. Many Hispanic Americans speak Spanish as their first language. Later they learn English.

Hernandez herself had a difficult experience as a child. When she started school, she spoke only Spanish. She was placed in a class with a teacher who spoke only English. She had to "sink or swim." It was hard until she finally learned enough English to get by.

So, Hernandez believes in bilingual education. The idea is to teach children in their native language first. They learn English on the side. Later they go on to regular classes taught only in English. At the same time, they continue to learn to read and write Spanish. This way they learn both languages well.

Bilingual education is controversial. It is a costly program. And some say it doesn't work any better than just putting children into regular classrooms. On the other hand, some say Spanish-speaking children should not have to give up their native language and culture.

Living in Washington, DC, has made Hernandez more aware of the different groups of Hispanic Americans. In Los Angeles where she grew up, most Hispanic Americans are Mexican. On the East Coast she has met Puerto Ricans, Cubans, and South and Central

Americans. This has given her a broader view of Hispanic Americans and their needs.

Hernandez has worked for unity among civil rights groups. She worked with the NAACP, the largest African-American civil rights group, on the 1992 Civil Rights Bill. She believes that all minority groups should work together for a stronger America.

In a July 8, 1991, issue of *Time* magazine, she is quoted as stating, "By acknowledging the contributions made to our country by Native Americans and by Hispanics and blacks and Asians, we're really strengthening our unity." Hernandez feels that all these groups have made vital contributions to what our country is today. And all these groups should be treated fairly and have equal rights.

Remembering the Facts

1. Of what civil rights group is Antonia Hernandez president?

2. What is the purpose of this group?

3. Where was Hernandez born?

4. Where did her family move when she was eight years old?

5. Why did Hernandez decide to change from teaching to law?

6. What kind of lawyer did Hernandez become after graduating from UCLA?

7. What Senate committee did Hernandez work on starting in 1978?

8. Why does Hernandez think bilingual education is important?

9. How did Hernandez get a broader view of who Hispanic Americans are?

10. How has Hernandez worked for unity among various civil rights groups?

Understanding the Story

11. Many people have very strong opinions for or against bilingual education. Why do you think it is such an emotional issue?

12. Why do you think Hernandez feels that all minority groups should work together? What would Native Americans, African Americans, Hispanic Americans, and Asians all have in common?

Getting the Main Idea

Why is Antonia Hernandez a good role model for young people today?

Applying What You've Learned

Imagine that you have been transferred to a school in another country. Your teacher and classmates do not speak English. And you do not speak a word of their language. Write a short explanation of how you would feel. How would you begin to understand their language? What would be your biggest frustrations?

Lupe Anguiano: Activist

Lupe Anguiano has dedicated her life to helping the poor and minorities. She has done this in many different ways.

Anguiano has been a teacher and a nun. She has worked as a counselor. She worked with President Johnson to improve education for Mexican Americans.

She worked with Cesar Chavez in *La Causa*. And she has worked to help poor women get the training they need to get off welfare.

Lupe Anguiano was born in 1929 in La Junta, Colorado. She was the fourth child of Mexican immigrants. Her father worked on the railroad.

Lupe Anguiano

In the summers, Anguiano's mother and all six children became migrant farmworkers. They went from farm to farm picking whatever crop was ready for harvest. Her father stayed behind to work on his railroad job all year round.

The family followed this pattern until Anguiano was thirteen. At this time they moved to Saticoy, California. They decided to stay there.

Up to this time, Anguiano had gone to school only once in a while. Her mother had taught her at home when there was time.

So, she started school at the age of thirteen, knowing how to read and write . . . in Spanish. Of course, school was taught in English. So, the first year was very hard for Anguiano. After that, things got better.

Anguiano went on to finish high school and junior college in Ventura, California. After graduation, she became a Catholic nun. For the next fifteen years she taught school.

Her last job as a nun was at a mission in Los Angeles. In this post she set up youth programs. She worked for better housing. And she worked to better the lives of the poor who lived near the mission.

Anguiano felt there were too many rules for nuns. She was not allowed to help the poor the way she hoped to. So, in 1964 she left the convent to work on her own.

She became a counselor. She worked with young people in East Los Angeles. She started Teen Post. This program helped young people aged thirteen to twenty.

In 1966 she was invited to the White House. President Lyndon Johnson wanted to know about the problems of Mexican Americans. She was asked to stay in Washington, DC. She set up a Mexican-American unit in the Department of Health, Education, and Welfare.

While in this post, Anguiano helped write the Bilingual Education Act. This act provided money to teach Spanish-speaking children in their native language as well as in English. The idea was that the children would learn to speak and read both languages well.

In practice, bilingual education turned out differently. The children learned English. But they were no longer taught any Spanish. Soon they had forgotten their Spanish. Anguiano was not happy with how the program was being run. So, she resigned her job with HEW.

It was 1968. The grape boycott led by Cesar Chavez was under way. Chavez was the head of the United Farm Workers. He asked Anguiano to work with him. So, she joined *La Causa*.

She walked on the picket lines. She led a grape boycott in Michigan. She remembers this work as the most rewarding thing she has ever done. Of Chavez, she says, "Cesar was the greatest man I have ever worked with!"

After the grape boycott's success, Anguiano took up another post with HEW. She was a civil rights specialist. Her job was to make sure that children who did not speak English got an equal chance for a good education.

While in this job, Anguiano became aware of the problems of women on welfare. She left HEW and went to San Antonio. There she began her Let's Get Off Welfare! campaign.

She organized the poor women of San Antonio. Some worked in day care for the children. Others went out and worked at other jobs.

The Let's Get Off Welfare! campaign worked because the whole community got behind it. Businesses offered to train women for jobs. Service clubs gave money to help with job training.

The program was highly successful. More than three thousand women were trained for jobs. Over ninety percent of these women then got jobs in the area of their training.

Women on welfare were given what they needed to better themselves. Job training and day care for their children helped them get on with their lives.

Not only that, it helped them feel better about themselves. The women were now able to take care of their families.

Anguiano continued to work on welfare reform. In 1979 she founded the National Women's Employment and Education Project. This group helped women on welfare get jobs. Nine model programs were set up in eight states. Some of these programs are still in place today.

Later, Anguiano started her own consulting firm. She helped businesses deal with problems relating to minority issues.

Today Anguiano still has her consulting business. She also hopes to write a book about welfare reform.

She continues to work for the acceptance of diversity in our country. Her dream is that one day all Americans—black, white, Hispanic, Asian, and Native American—will work together for a stronger America.

Remembering the Facts

1. Where was Lupe Anguiano born?

2. How did the family earn money in the summers?

3. Why was school difficult at first for Anguiano?

4. What did Anguiano do when she finished junior college?

5. Why was she invited to the White House by President Johnson?

6. What was the purpose of the Bilingual Education Act?

7. Why was Anguiano unhappy with the way the bilingual education program was being run?

8. What work did Anguiano do with Cesar Chavez in 1968?

9. How did the Let's Get Off Welfare! campaign help women get off welfare?

10. What type of work is Anguiano doing today?

Understanding the Story

11. Lupe Anguiano has done a wide variety of work in her lifetime. What do you see as the common thread that runs throughout her life?

12. Anguiano believes that the welfare program needs to be changed. She believes that poor women with children need job training and good child care. Why do you think this could help them more than just giving them money?

Getting the Main Idea

Why do you think Lupe Anguiano would be a good role model for the youth of today?

Applying What You've Learned

Anguiano has been called both a dreamer and a realist. Why do you think both qualities are important for a leader? Write a paragraph explaining your answer.

Henry B. Gonzalez: U.S. Congressman

Henry B. Gonzalez is a United States Representative from the state of Texas. He has held this job since 1961. Gonzalez was the first Mexican American to be elected to Congress.

In 1953 Gonzalez decided to run for the city council of San Antonio. He went to the city leaders and asked for their help. Every one of them told Gonzalez not to run. The reason? "A Mexican cannot win," they told him.

But Gonzalez was stubborn. He did run. And he *was* elected to the city council.

Later he decided to run for the Texas state senate. Again he was told that a Mexican could not win a state office.

Henry B. Gonzalez

But he won that race too. That made him the first Mexican American in one hundred years to be elected to the state senate.

Gonzalez did not stop there. In 1961 he ran for the United States Congress. He won fifty-five percent of the vote. That was a major victory.

63

In those days the voting rights of African Americans and Hispanics were restricted. So, it was clear that many white Texans must have voted for Gonzalez. It was an amazing victory for Henry B. Gonzalez.

Henry Barbosa Gonzalez was born in 1916 in San Antonio, Texas. He was one of six children.

Gonzalez's father had been the mayor of Mapimi, a village in northern Mexico. During the 1910 Revolution he was forced to flee his home. He went to San Antonio. He became the editor of *La Prensa*. This was the only newspaper written in Spanish in the United States.

Gonzalez grew up in a home that was full of talk of politics and ideas. Both parents stressed the importance of a good education. From an early age, Henry loved to read. The public library was his second home.

But Gonzalez had problems in school. To begin with, his family spoke only Spanish in their home. So Gonzalez reached school age without knowing a word of English.

When it was time for him to start school, his father had to drag him out of the house. In class he was one of a handful of Mexican-American children. He was so frightened he didn't speak a word for months. But by the end of the year he had learned English and was on his way.

Gonzalez graduated from Thomas Jefferson High School. He went on to college. He earned a law degree from St. Mary's University School of Law in 1943.

But Gonzalez never practiced law. He worked for a Spanish-English translation service for a few years. He worked on housing programs in San Antonio. During World War II, he worked for army intelligence.

As a state senator, Gonzalez fought for minority rights. He worked for programs to replace slums with better housing. He was against a sales tax that would have hurt the poor.

He was famous for his filibusters. In fact, he set a state record for the longest filibuster. A filibuster is a long speech. It is used to delay a bill coming up for a vote.

At the time, the Texas state senate was trying to pass a set of ten racial segregation bills. Gonzalez and another senator filibustered for thirty-six hours.

After speaking for twenty-two hours, Gonzalez said, "I have seen the effects of segregation firsthand for many years. If we fear long enough, we hate. And if we hate long enough, we fight. If a bill violates the rights of even one person, then it has to be struck down." Only one of the ten bills was passed.

Gonzalez was a close friend of President John F. Kennedy. On November 22, 1963, Gonzalez was with Kennedy on a trip to Dallas. Just before they got off the plane, Gonzalez joked, "I'm taking my risks. I haven't got my steel vest on." Just minutes later, while riding into Dallas, President Kennedy was shot and killed.

Gonzalez suspected that Kennedy's assassin had not acted alone. He asked Congress to look into the case. He also wanted the assassination of Dr. Martin Luther King, Jr., investigated.

In 1981 Gonzalez became chairman of the House Banking Subcommittee on Housing. He pushed hard for more low-income housing. He finally got the Affordable Housing Act passed in 1990. This act helps low-income families to buy homes.

In 1988 Gonzalez became chairman of the House Banking, Finance, and Urban Affairs Committee. His first task was to handle the savings and loan crisis. A savings and loan is a type of bank that lends money for home buying.

The head of one savings and loan had tried to bribe several U.S. senators. Some savings and loans were guilty of fraud. Others were not managing their money the right way.

Gonzalez got a bill passed to bail out some failing savings and loans. Then he set up tighter rules for how they could do business. Stricter laws for regular banks were set up too.

In all the years he has been in Congress, Gonzalez has always been known for his honesty and independence. Gonzalez himself once said, "I walked through the mud of San Antonio politics. I walked through the mud of state politics in Texas. And for thirty years, I've walked through the mud in Washington, DC, and I still haven't gotten the tips of my shoes dirty." Henry B. Gonzalez is his own man.6

In San Antonio, he is a hero. As a matter of fact, he is so popular that he has been reelected to Congress seventeen times, as of 1994. Six of those times he ran unopposed. Henry B., as he is known, has almost saintlike status in his home state.

Remembering the Facts

1. What job has Henry B. Gonzalez held since 1961?

2. Where was Gonzalez born?

3. Why did Gonzalez have trouble when he started school?

4. What kind of degree did Gonzalez earn from St. Mary's University?

5. Name two things Gonzalez worked for while in the Texas state senate.

    a.

    b.

6. How did Gonzalez bring nine out of ten segregationist bills to defeat?

7. With which U.S. president was Gonzalez close friends?

8. What law did Gonzalez get passed when he was chairman of the House Banking Subcommittee on Housing?

9. What was the first crisis Gonzalez had to handle as chairman of the House Banking, Finance, and Urban Affairs Committee?

10. What kind of reputation does Gonzalez have in Washington, DC?

Understanding the Story

11. Henry B., as he is known by many, is very popular in his home state of Texas. Why do you think he is so well liked?

12. Explain this statement by Gonzalez: "And for thirty years, I've walked through the mud in Washington, DC, and I still haven't gotten the tips of my shoes dirty."

Getting the Main Idea

Why do you think Henry B. Gonzalez is a good role model for the youth of today?

Applying What You've Learned

Draw a political cartoon. Show Henry B. Gonzalez fighting for one of his causes. Use an example from the story. Or make up an example showing a cause you think Gonzalez would favor.

Roberto Goizueta: Chairman of the Coca-Cola Company

Roberto Goizueta

There are few Cuban Americans in the top ranks of business. One of the few is Roberto Goizueta. He became chairman and chief executive of the Coca-Cola Company in 1980.

Goizueta has led the company to new highs in sales. Coca-Cola is now America's sixth most valuable public company.

Roberto Goizueta was born in Havana, Cuba, in 1931. His father was a businessman. Goizueta grew up in a wealthy home.

At the age of eighteen, Goizueta came to the United States. He went to a private high school.

Goizueta didn't know a word of English. A year later he could speak English well. He learned "after many sleepless nights studying the dictionary."

Because he was so rich, his classmates thought he might be spoiled. They were wrong. Goizueta was a hard worker. He had good values. He finished high school first in his class.

Goizueta went on to Yale. He graduated in 1954. He got a job as a chemist at the Coca-Cola plant in Havana, Cuba.

Then Fidel Castro came to power in Cuba. The country became communist. By 1960 Castro was taking over businesses and property. Many people were thrown in jail for little or no reason.

So, Goizueta and his family fled Cuba in 1961. Shortly after, the government of Cuba took over the Coca-Cola plant there.

For the next twenty-six years, Goizueta made his way up the ladder at Coca-Cola. He worked on the island of Nassau. He became the head of Coca-Cola's Caribbean office. Soon he was second in command over all of Latin America.

In 1965 he moved to Atlanta, Georgia. Atlanta is the site of the company's main offices. He became Coca-Cola's youngest vice president ever. In 1980 he was named head of the whole company.

Some people were not happy when Goizueta was put in charge. He was only forty-eight. There were older and more experienced people in line for the job.

Other people did not like the fact that Goizueta had come from Cuba. He spoke English well, but he spoke it with a heavy accent. How could such a man lead the all-American company Coca-Cola?

In the end Goizueta's Cuban background was helpful. Two thirds of the sales of Coke® are outside the United States. Speaking two languages turned out to be a plus.

Over the next five years, Goizueta led the company to an all-time high in sales and profits. The company chose a new slogan:

"Coke Is It!" Indeed, one out of every three soft drinks sold in the United States was a Coke.

All this success was not due to sales of Coke. It was also due to a new product that came out in 1982: Diet Coke®.

Coke itself was losing ground to Pepsi. Goizueta needed to boost Coke's sales. But what he did shocked America to its very core. He said that he was changing Coke to make it taste "better." The new Coke was sweeter, smoother. In fact it tasted more like Pepsi®.

People all across the country were upset. The Coca-Cola company received thousands of calls a day. No one could believe that Coke had been changed. Coke was an American tradition. One man said that changing Coke was like making grass purple!

It took just a month for Goizueta to get the message from the American people. "We want our Coke back!" So, he said that from then on there would be two Cokes: new Coke and old Coke. The old Coke was called Coca-Cola Classic.

New Coke had been a big mistake. But it turned out all right in the end. There were two Cokes. And Coca-Cola was selling more soft drinks than ever. (Today, new Coke is no longer sold. But Coke still sells more soft drinks than anyone else.)

But how did Coca-Cola itself get its start? Let's look back to the year 1886 and see. Coke was invented in Atlanta, Georgia, by John Pemberton. Mr. Pemberton was a druggist. He sold his new drink in his drugstore soda fountain.

Pemberton sold his business to Asa Candler. Candler sent salesmen across America with kegs of Coke syrup and instructions for mixing up the drink. At this time, it was still only sold in soda fountains.

Candler also began advertising Coke. Coca-Cola signs were painted on barns across America. By 1895 Coke was being sold in every state. It was one of the first brand-name foods to be sold nationwide.

Next Candler began selling Coke syrup to local bottlers across the country. All bottlers had to buy the syrup from Coca-Cola. Then they mixed and bottled the drink for sale. That is the way Coke is still made today. Candler sold the company to the Woodruff family. Robert Woodruff became the new head.

It was World War II that gave Coca-Cola its international fame. Woodruff said he would see that every soldier could get a Coke for five cents. It did not matter where he was or how much it cost the company. Woodruff got the American government to help set up bottling plants worldwide. At home, ads linked Coke with the war effort.

By the end of the war, Coca-Cola was the most popular soft drink in America. It had become a symbol of patriotism. It had become a symbol of America.

Today Coke has spread throughout the world. It is sold in nearly every country. (Cuba is not one of them.) The Coca-Cola Company holds nearly 50 percent of the world market in soft drinks.

Goizueta has put Coca-Cola on top of the soft drink world. And at sixty-three he has no plans to retire soon. He loves his work, often putting in ten-hour days. "Coke Is It!" for Roberto Goizueta.

Remembering the Facts

1. Where was Roberto Goizueta born?

2. What problem did he have to overcome when he came to America at the age of eighteen?

3. Why did the Goizueta family leave Cuba in 1961?

4. What job did Goizueta get in 1980?

5. Why were some people unhappy when Goizueta took over the company?

6. What was the biggest marketing mistake made by Goizueta?

7. How was this marketing mistake corrected?

8. Where and when was Coca-Cola invented?

9. Why did Coke go international during World War II?

10. What percentage of the world's soft drink market is held by Coca-Cola?

Understanding the Story

11. Why do you think Coke became a symbol of patriotism, of America, and of the free-market system?

12. Why do you think people were so upset when Coca-Cola changed its formula in 1984?

Getting the Main Idea

Why do you think Roberto Goizueta is a good role model for the youth of today?

Applying What You've Learned

Think of a new slogan to replace the "Coke Is It!" slogan. Design a poster featuring the new slogan. Your poster should appeal to teenagers and young adults.

Rita Moreno:
Actress

Rita Moreno

Rita Moreno is in the *Guinness Book of World Records.* She is the only person who has won all four of the big awards for performers.

First, Moreno won an Oscar. She won for best supporting actress in the movie *West Side Story.* She won a Tony award for the Broadway play *The Ritz.*

A Grammy award was hers for an album of songs from *The Electric Company.* And she has won two Emmy awards for television shows.

Rita Moreno is a talented actress. She is also a great dancer and singer. But she has had to work very hard to overcome prejudice and make her success.

Rita Moreno was born in 1931 in Puerto Rico. Her parents divorced soon after she was born.

Moreno's mother went to New York. She left young Rita with her family in Puerto Rico while she worked as a seamstress. When Moreno was five years old, her mother had saved enough money to return for her. Together, they went back to New York. They lived in a poor part of town.

Moreno went to New York Public School 132. She started taking dancing lessons. Soon she was dancing for a living. Her earnings helped her family get by. By the age of thirteen, she had quit school to work full-time.

At the age of nineteen she got a contract with MGM studios. She played small parts in several movies. Then she lost her contract.

Moreno found movie parts on her own. Moreno was always typecast in B-grade movies. That means in each movie she played the same type of character. She called these her "Latin spitfire" roles.

These roles became a problem for her. Directors called her when they wanted to cast a "Latin type." They did not see her talent. They only saw she was Hispanic.

In 1955 Moreno got a break. She played a slave girl in the hit *The King and I*. Moreno thinks of this as her best movie of the 1950's. For her part in this movie, she got strong reviews.

In 1961 Moreno starred in the movie for which she is most famous: *West Side Story*. This movie earned ten Academy Awards. One of these was the best supporting actress award for Rita Moreno. She stole the show with her singing and dancing. At last it was clear she was a first-rate talent.

She did many more movies over the next ten years. Again, she received good reviews.

In 1964 she married Dr. Leonard Gordon. They had one daughter.

In 1971 a change of pace came up. Moreno was asked to star in *The Electric Company.* This was a children's series on PBS. It taught reading to children ages seven to ten.

Moreno was thrilled. She loved doing an educational show. The series was fun too. She played a variety of funny characters. None of them were Hispanic. In 1972 she and Bill Cosby won a Grammy award for a recording of some of the songs from the show.

In 1975 Rita Moreno played the part of Googie Gomez in the Broadway play *The Ritz.* Gomez was a Puerto Rican singer. In this role Moreno made fun of the silly roles she had been forced to play for so many years.

Moreno was a hit. It was a surprise to no one when she won the Tony award for the best supporting actress. The play ran for 400 performances. Audiences loved it.

In 1977 she did guest appearances on *The Muppet Show.* For this work she won an Emmy award. She won another Emmy in 1978 for an episode of *The Rockford Files.*

In 1982 and 1983 Moreno starred in a TV series called *Nine to Five.* This comedy was about the rights of working women.

During the last ten years, Moreno has played on Broadway. She has performed in theaters around the United States.

Moreno is now known as a talented actor, singer, and dancer. Today she is in her sixties. But she still wows audiences with her dancing and singing. In fact, she has recently done an exercise video for older women, called *Now You Can.* She also co-starred in a 1995 television series with Bill Cosby (*The Cosby Mysteries*).

Moreno wants to work for the Hispanic community. She hopes to be a role model for young Hispanic women. She hopes her life will show how prejudice and poverty can be overcome.

In 1989 Moreno won a Woman of the Year award from *Hispanic* magazine. At that time she spoke of her pride in being a Hispanic American.

She told the magazine, "I have learned how essential it is to cling to one's own heritage, for only in that way can we truly understand our culture . . . and ourselves."

Remembering the Facts

1. Why is Rita Moreno in the *Guinness Book of World Records?*

2. Where was Moreno born?

3. What type of roles did she play in her early career?

4. Why did these roles create a problem for her?

5. What 1955 movie does Moreno consider her best movie role of the 1950's?

6. For what movie did Moreno win an Academy Award?

7. Moreno won a Grammy award for a recording of songs from what children's TV show?

8. What was the name of the Broadway play for which Moreno won a Tony award?

9. Name one TV show for which Moreno won an Emmy award.

Understanding the Story

10. In her early career Moreno did twenty-five movies for MGM, which cast her in stereotyped Hispanic roles. Why do you think she had trouble getting any other kind of part? Do you think a young Hispanic actress today would have the same kind of trouble?

11. In an interview for *Hispanic* magazine, Moreno said, "I have learned how essential it is to cling to one's own heritage, for only in that way can we truly understand our culture . . . and ourselves." Do you agree with Moreno? Why or why not?

Getting the Main Idea

Why do you think Rita Moreno is a good role model for young people of today?

Applying What You've Learned

Imagine that you are a graphic artist. Rita Moreno is coming to your town to do a performance. You have been assigned to do a poster to advertise the event. Decide what type of performance Moreno will be doing. Design a poster to advertise the event. Use information from the story to help you.

Antonia Novello: Surgeon General

Antonia Novello was the fourteenth surgeon general of the United States. She was the first woman to hold that job. She was also the first Hispanic and the first Puerto Rican to be the nation's "first doctor."

Antonia Novello was born in 1944 in Puerto Rico. Her father died when she was eight years old. Novello grew up poor.

Novello met many doctors when she was very young. She was born with a large intestine that did not work well. So she was often ill. Every year she spent at least two weeks in the hospital.

Antonia Novello

Surgery could have fixed the problem. But she was not able to get it until she was eighteen. Novello says that's the main reason she became a doctor. She hoped to be able to help others get the care they need *when they need it.*

Novello's doctors were her heroes as a child. She dreamed of one day becoming a doctor for children.

Novello went to the University of Puerto Rico to study medicine. In 1970 her dream came true: She became an M.D.

Novello was an intern and resident at University of Michigan Medical Center. Then she studied at Georgetown University Hospital in Washington, DC. She also got a master's degree in public health from Johns Hopkins University in Baltimore.

In 1976 Novello opened an office. She began work as a pediatrician. A few years later, she decided the work did not suit her. She said, "When the pediatrician cries as much as the parents of the patients do, then you know it's time to get out."

Novello went to work for the public health service. She rose quickly through the ranks. She worked with the United States Congress on health-related issues.

In 1989 President George Bush nominated Novello to be the surgeon general. She was confirmed by the Senate. On March 9, 1990, she became the nation's fourteenth surgeon general. Her oath of office was given by another "first," Justice Sandra Day O'Connor, the first woman on the U.S. Supreme Court.

As surgeon general, Novello's job was to protect the health of the American people. She asked for research on major health problems. She warned the public about dangers to their health. She also headed the public health service.

Novello focused on health care for children, women, and minorities. She was concerned about violence and child abuse. Alcohol and drug use were another main concern.

Novello thought all Americans should have good health care. She focused on those "who cannot speak up for themselves." This includes children and teenagers.

Every surgeon general has his or her ideas for which programs should be given top priority. Antonia Novello chose four areas she would emphasize during her term of office. These were alcohol, tobacco, AIDS, and violence. Let's look at her views on these issues.

Alcohol

Novello attacked alcohol ads. She said they send kids the wrong message about alcohol. The ads make drinking look like the "key to fun and a wonderful and carefree lifestyle."

Novello worked for a ban on alcohol ads targeting young people. She asked for more alcohol education in schools.

Novello said alcohol is a big problem facing America's youth. At least eight million underage students drink alcohol. At least half a million are alcoholics.

Alcohol can cause health problems in a growing body. Drinking and driving puts lives at risk. Over half of all violent crimes involve alcohol use.

Seventy percent of suicides involve alcohol use. In fifty percent of drownings, the victim has been drinking. Injuries from falls, shootings, and fires are also often alcohol related.

Tobacco

Another of Novello's targets was tobacco companies. Novello said that ninety percent of adults who smoke began smoking in their teens. Everyone knows smoking is bad for one's health. But millions of teenagers smoke.

Novello said tobacco ads are aimed at the young. One study showed that ninety-one percent of six-year-olds knew that the cartoon figure Joe Camel sells cigarettes. The Marlboro Man ads show smokers as strong and independent. Novello asked tobacco companies to stop ads that appeal to those under eighteen.

AIDS

Novello stressed AIDS education. Everyone must know how to protect themselves from AIDS.

Violence

Novello said violence is a major public health problem. Fifty thousand persons are murdered in the United States each year. Among African-American youth, murder is the leading cause of death.

Violence affects low-income and minority groups more than other groups. But it affects all of us, filling our lives with fear.

Abuse of women and children is another kind of violence that is growing. We need to teach our children that violence is not a good way to handle problems. There must be help for abusers and their victims.

✻ ✻ ✻ ✻ ✻ ✻ ✻ ✻

During her term as surgeon general, Antonia Novello made no secret of her special concern for America's children. She decorated her office with Cabbage Patch dolls. She had children's artwork on the walls. Often she made time to visit children in hospitals.

Antonia Novello's motto is "Good science, good sense." She hoped that by making good sense in her public health campaigns, people would listen. And after listening, they would make changes for a healthier life.

Remembering the Facts

1. What "firsts" did Antonia Novello make when she became the nation's "first doctor"?

    a.

    b.

    c.

2. Where was Antonia Novello born?

3. Why did Novello become interested in becoming a doctor?

4. What is the job of the surgeon general?

5. What two things did Novello do to stop alcohol use among the young?

    a.

    b.

6. What did she do about tobacco use among the young?

7. Name three other issues Novello was concerned about as surgeon general.

    a.

    b.

    c.

Understanding the Story

8. Why do you think Antonia Novello focused so much of her work as surgeon general on the problems of young people?

9. Why do you think Novello talked so much about alcohol and tobacco use by the young? Do you think she was right to put so much emphasis on these topics? Why or why not?

Getting the Main Idea

Why do you think Antonia Novello would be a good role model for young people of today?

Applying What You've Learned

Make a collection of ads for alcohol and tobacco products. You may cut ads out of newspapers or magazines. Or write a summary (a few sentences) telling about ads you've seen. For each ad in your collection, tell how the ad tries to make smoking or drinking look appealing.

José Feliciano:
Singer

José Feliciano

José Feliciano was born in Puerto Rico in 1945. He was the second of twelve children born to a poor farmer.

Feliciano's father could not make a go of it farming. So the family moved to New York City when José was five years old. They lived in a ghetto called Spanish Harlem.

The family was poor. But José had a bigger problem. He had been born blind.

Feliciano was not allowed to join the street games played by other children. He spent much time at home by himself. He filled his time listening to the radio. Singers became his childhood heroes.

Feliciano remembers using a tin cracker can as a drum at the age of three. By six, he had taught himself to play the accordion. He played the same record over and over. Then he figured out how to make the same sounds on his instrument.

By the age of eight, Feliciano had taught himself to play the guitar. Again, he used a handful of records as his guide. He practiced fourteen hours a day.

When he was nine, he began performing in public. His first job was at a theater in Spanish Harlem. Feliciano was very small. His father had to pick him up so the crowd could see him.

Times were hard for the Feliciano family. When José was seventeen, his father lost his job. José quit school to help earn money. He played wherever he could. Afterward he would pass the hat.

It was not easy for him to get jobs at first. So, he thought of a trick. He would ask coffeehouse managers if they would listen to him sing. Most of them said "no." They knew nothing about him.

Then Feliciano would ask if he could tune his guitar before he left. The managers could not turn down that request. Of course, the guitar would already be in tune. Feliciano would pull it out and play beautifully. Often he would be hired.

Feliciano began to gain a following among folk music lovers in New York City. Soon he was playing at some of the better known clubs.

Feliciano was only seventeen when he got his big break. He was playing in a club in Greenwich Village. A man from RCA records was visiting the club to hear another act. He heard Feliciano instead. He wasted no time in signing the young man.

During the next five years, Feliciano made records in Spanish. These were for the Latin American market. He toured Europe, Central America, and South America. He became very popular among Spanish-speaking people. He even had his own Spanish language TV show. This show was shown all over Latin America.

Feliciano was a major recording artist in Latin America before he hit the U.S. charts. His hit album *Feliciano!* zoomed to the top of the charts in 1968. The single "Light My Fire" was the number one single in 1968. Both earned a gold record that same year.

By the end of 1968, Feliciano was a star in the United States as well. He appeared on almost every major TV show. And he starred in several of his own television specials.

In 1968 Feliciano became the first person to put his own spin on the national anthem during a sports event. He had been asked to sing "The Star-Spangled Banner" to open the fifth game of the 1968 World Series. He chose to do it in a "Spanish soul" style.

Many people were upset. They couldn't believe that he dared to sing the national anthem in such a way. In fact many radio stations quit playing his records in protest. Other people loved it. But for the first time, the national anthem (Feliciano style) was on the record charts.

Feliciano's biggest hits have featured him singing. But he is equally known for his skill on the guitar. He has played his guitar with the London Symphony and the Los Angeles Philharmonic.

Feliciano is a rare artist. Besides the guitar, he plays the bass, banjo, and keyboard. He plays the harmonica, the mandolin, and the timbales. He also plays the piano, the organ, and the bongos.

He sings rock 'n roll and blues. He sings folk and Latin-American music. And he sings in seven different languages.

Today Feliciano still works hard at his music. Concert tours and recording sessions take most of his time.

Every year he does a Valentine's Day concert in his native Puerto Rico. People there love him, and he returns the feeling.

People all over the world have been charmed by Feliciano. He was one of the first Western stars to perform in Russia. For that show, he even learned to do some songs in Russian.

Feliciano has had over forty gold and platinum records so far in his career. And he has won six Grammy awards.

But Feliciano feels as if his career is just beginning. After all, he has a whole new generation of listeners. He feels that he is just beginning to share his music with the world.

Feliciano says that hard work is the "magic" ingredient toward success in any field. Feliciano says, "You can make it in music if you give it everything you've got and make sure it's the only thing on your mind." If you listen to his music, you will know he gives it all he's got. Feliciano says that music still gives him the same happiness it did when he was a child.

The name Feliciano means "the happy one" in Spanish. He has lived his life with a positive can-do attitude, in spite of the handicap he had at birth—being born blind into a poor family. Through his music he has also given happiness to millions around the world.

Remembering the Facts

1. Where was Feliciano born?

2. What two handicaps did Feliciano have to overcome?

   a.

   b.

3. How did Feliciano get jobs at coffeehouses at first?

4. How did Feliciano get his big break?

5. Where did Feliciano gain fame before he became known in the United States?

6. Name the hit single that sent Feliciano to the top of the record charts in the United States.

7. Feliciano plays many instruments. But he is best known for his skill on which instrument?

8. Where does Feliciano play a Valentine's Day concert every year?

9. What does Feliciano say is the way to success in any field?

10. What does the name Feliciano mean in Spanish?

Understanding the Story

11. In 1968 Feliciano was the first person to sing the national anthem in a nontraditional way. (Since then many singers have done so.) Why do you think so many people were upset? Do you think it is OK for performers to sing "The Star-Spangled Banner" however they want?

12. Because he was blind, Feliciano had many lonely hours to fill as a child. So he turned to music. Do you think he would still have developed his talent if he had *not* been blind? Why or why not?

Getting the Main Idea

Why do you think José Feliciano is a good role model for the youth of today?

Applying What You've Learned

Design a poster to advertise an upcoming Feliciano concert in your area. Use facts from the story on your poster.

Ileana Ros-Lehtinen: U.S. Representative

Ileana Ros-Lehtinen is used to being first! In 1982 she was the first Cuban-American woman to win election to the Florida state legislature.

In 1989 she was the first Cuban-American woman to be elected to the United States Congress. She was also the first Hispanic-American woman to win this post.

As a U.S. Representative, Ros-Lehtinen can work for all Cuban Americans. But she wants to represent all the people of her district.

Ileana Ros-Lehtinen was born in 1952 in Havana, Cuba. Her father was an accountant.

The Ros family lived a pleasant life. Then Fidel Castro came to power. Like many others, the Ros family fled to Miami in 1960. They left behind their home and all they owned.

Ileana Ros-Lehtinen

There were many Cuban exiles in Miami. They all hoped that Castro would not stay in power long. Groups of exiles gathered at the Ros home nightly. They plotted ways to overthrow Castro. Then they would be able to go back to Cuba. Ileana Ros-Lehtinen remembers her home being "like a camp, full of people all day."

But it soon became clear that things in Cuba were not going to get better anytime soon. Ros's parents decided that they would raise their children as Americans. They thought it wasn't fair to raise them without knowing which country they belonged to. Mr. Ros said, "This is going to be their country, and they should love it!"

So it was no surprise that Ileana Ros developed a strong desire to serve her country. She lost her native land to communism. So she takes democracy very seriously.

Ileana Ros-Lehtinen graduated from Miami-Dade County Community College in 1972. She earned a degree in English from Florida International University in 1975. Later she earned a master's degree in educational leadership there.

Ros-Lehtinen became a teacher. She founded her own private school, Eastern Academy. She was the principal of the school for ten years.

Ros-Lehtinen has always loved politics. When she was a child, her parents taught her to love democracy. So it was natural that she would run for the Florida state legislature. She ran and won.

From 1982 to 1986 she was a state representative. Then she was a state senator until 1989.

While in the legislature, she met her future husband, Dexter Lehtinen. He was also a state senator.

In 1989 the popular longtime U.S. Congressman Claude Pepper died. A special election was held to fill his seat.

Ileana Ros-Lehtinen, a Republican, ran against Democrat Gerald Richman. It ended up being a bitter race.

The problems began when the Republican national chairman said that since the district was fifty percent Cuban, it was important to elect a Cuban American to the job. To this, Richman reportedly answered, "This is an American seat."

Many Cuban Americans in Miami were upset by this remark. It sounded to them as if Richman was saying that they were not real Americans.

So over ninety percent of the Hispanic-American vote went to Ros-Lehtinen. Most of the whites and African Americans voted for Richman. But in the end Ros-Lehtinen got fifty-three percent of the vote. She was the new congresswoman from Florida's 18th District. Her election showed how powerful the Cuban-American vote had become in Florida.

In her victory speech, Ros-Lehtinen said she would start working to heal the wounds caused by the campaign. During her speech she suddenly switched from English to Spanish. She did this to show those listening to her in Cuba what a democracy was all about.

Ros-Lehtinen worked hard for all the people in her district. In 1990 she was reelected with sixty percent of the vote. She was also reelected in 1992. In 1994 she ran unopposed and got one hundred percent of the vote.

She is well liked in her district because she spends most of her time helping local voters. Her office helps people with such things as getting food stamps or immigration papers.

Ros-Lehtinen feels that service to the people of her district is the most important part of her job in Congress. She sees herself as a middle person between the voter and the government. This approach has brought her a loyal following in her district.

In Congress, Ros-Lehtinen has served on the Foreign Affairs Committee. She has also worked on the Employment and Housing Subcommittee.

She supports bilingual education. She is for a seven-day waiting period to buy a handgun. She also favors tough sentences for drug dealers.

Like most Cuban Americans, Ros-Lehtinen is a strong opponent of Fidel Castro. She hopes that one day Cuba will again be a democracy.

In 1991 the Pan American Games were held in Cuba. The games are an international sports contest much like the Olympics. Ros-Lehtinen asked athletes not to participate in the games.

In 1992 Ileana Ros-Lehtinen was presented with an award for outstanding achievement from *Hispanic* magazine. She hopes to be a good role model for other Hispanic women. By seeing her achievements, they will know that they too can succeed at those things they really want to do.

Remembering the Facts

1. What "first" did Ros-Lehtinen achieve in 1982?

2. What "first" did she achieve in 1989?

3. Where was Ros-Lehtinen born?

4. Why did the Ros family leave Cuba?

5.   How did Ros-Lehtinen's parents give her a strong desire to serve her country?

6.   What did Ros-Lehtinen train to be when she was in college?

7.   Why were Cuban-American voters upset by the remark, "This is an American (congressional) seat"?

8.   How did the vote in the 1989 election split along racial and ethnic lines?

9.   Name one issue supported by Ros-Lehtinen.

10.   What is Ros-Lehtinen's opinion of Fidel Castro?

Understanding the Story

11.   Why do you think Ileana Ros-Lehtinen is such a strong opponent of Fidel Castro and his government?

12.   If Castro were no longer in power and Cuba became a democracy, do you think Ros-Lehtinen and other Cuban Americans would return to Cuba to live? Why or why not?

Getting the Main Idea

Why is Ileana Ros-Lehtinen a good role model for the youth of today?

Applying What You've Learned

Imagine that you are a Cuban American living in Miami in 1989. The congressional race between Ileana Ros-Lehtinen and Gerald Richman is in full swing. One day you read in your newspaper a remark attributed to Richman: "This is an American (congressional) seat."

Write a letter to the editor in which you express your opinion about this statement.

Background Information

Who are the Hispanic Americans?

The United States government defines "Hispanics" as people who speak Spanish or who are of Spanish, Portuguese, or Latin American (Central or South American) descent. The three largest groups are Mexican Americans, Puerto Ricans, and Cubans.

Just as there is a wide variety of Hispanic groups, there is a variety of terms these groups use to refer to themselves. The term *Hispanic* is a general term that includes all these groups.

Some prefer the term *Latino* instead of *Hispanic*. Other Hispanic Americans refer to themselves by their particular group—that is, Cuban American, Mexican American, Puerto Rican, etc. Some Mexican Americans prefer the term *Chicano*.

In this book we have chosen to use the broader term *Hispanic American* to refer to all those with Spanish ancestry.

How many Americans are Hispanic?

The 1990 census showed there were 22,400,000 Hispanic Americans in the United States. (That is 9 percent of the country's total population of 240 million.) The census bureau estimates there will be 30 million Hispanics by the year 2000 and 40 million by 2010. At that point there will be an equal number of Hispanics and African Americans (each 13 percent of the population).

The Hispanic population is increasing quickly. Half of the population increase is due to immigration, mostly from Mexico. A second reason is the high birthrate among Hispanics.

99

Where do Hispanic Americans Live?

Most Mexican Americans live in Texas, New Mexico, Colorado, Arizona, and California. Puerto Ricans live mostly in New York, New Jersey, and Illinois. Most Cubans live in Florida.

In 1990 almost two thirds of Hispanic Americans lived in twenty-five large U.S. cities. In Los Angeles County there are 3 million Hispanic Americans. That makes Los Angeles the second largest Spanish-speaking city in the world! (Mexico City is the largest.)

Why are so many countries Spanish-speaking?

Spain at one time was a superpower in the world. Spaniards put much energy into exploring and conquering new parts of the world, settling much of North and South America. In 1492 Columbus landed in America. The first Spanish settlement in North America was at St. Augustine, Florida, in 1563.

In Mexico the Spanish conquered the native Indians. Intermarriage over the years produced the Mexican people (*mestizo*). Thus, the heritage of Mexicans is both Indian and Spanish.

Cuba and Puerto Rico were conquered by the Spanish as well. The Spanish forced the native Indians into slavery. They also imported many African slaves. Thus, Cubans and Puerto Ricans have a Spanish, Indian, and African heritage.

Why did Mexicans immigrate to the United States?

Many Mexicans became U.S. citizens in the 1800's. In 1821 Mexico declared its independence from Spain. Then in 1848 Mexico lost the Mexican War to the United States. It was forced to give the U.S. the northern half of its holdings, including what is now California, Arizona, Utah, and Nevada. At that time the Mexicans living there were given the choice of becoming U.S. citizens or returning to Mexico. Eighty percent stayed and became U.S. citizens. Later, additional territory was purchased from Mexico, becoming parts of Arizona and New Mexico. Many Mexican residents of this land became U.S. citizens as well.

In the late 1800's many more Mexicans came north seeking jobs as the Mexican economy weakened. They worked as farm and ranch hands, railroad workers and miners, and factory workers. Today thousands of Mexicans continue to migrate north each year seeking work. Thus there are always many Mexican immigrants, both legal and illegal.

Why did Cubans immigrate to the United States?

Before 1959 there were few Cuban immigrants. But in 1959 Fidel Castro overthrew the Cuban government and declared Cuba a communist state. He outlawed individual ownership of property and accumulation of wealth. Many middle- and upper-class Cubans fled Cuba. Castro allowed them to take only the clothes on their backs and five dollars in American money. The Cuban government took the rest of their wealth. Most of these people ended up in Miami, Florida. They were mainly educated professional people who were welcomed into the United States.

A second large group of Cubans was allowed to leave Cuba in 1980. This "boat-lift" of Cubans was controversial because, unlike the first group, most of these people were from the lower class. A number were even criminals or mentally ill individuals that Castro wanted to get rid of. These immigrants were not particularly welcomed by the first group of Cubans or by white Miamians.

The number of Cubans in the U.S. rose from 30,000 in 1959 to 1.1 million in 1991. Cubans are a major force in Florida, especially in Miami.

Why did Puerto Ricans immigrate to the United States?

In 1898, following the Spanish-American War, Puerto Rico became a possession of the U.S., and in 1917 Puerto Ricans were granted U.S. citizenship. Since that time, Puerto Ricans have had the unrestricted right to travel between the island and the mainland. After World War II the economy of Puerto Rico began to weaken. Many Puerto Ricans have migrated to the U.S. since then. In 1991 there were about 2.4 million Puerto Ricans living in the U.S. Most of these live in New York City. About 3.5 million other Puerto Ricans live on the island of Puerto Rico.

What other countries do Hispanics come from?

Immigrants come from Latin American countries such as Nicaragua, Guatemala, Honduras, Colombia, Dominican Republic, and El Salvador. Most come to escape civil war, poverty, and political repression.

The 1969 border war between Honduras and El Salvador caused economic conditions to deteriorate in all of Central America. Civil wars and unrest in Guatemala, El Salvador, and Nicaragua since 1979 have caused large migrations. The number of Central and South Americans in the United States has been estimated at about 1.5 million.

Key Vocabulary

Cesar Chavez

La Causa	civil rights	nonviolent protest
migrant workers	register to vote	union
strike	*huelga*	boycott
pesticides		

Joan Baez

Quakers	nonviolence	dyslexic
folk music	debut	soprano
discrimination	drafted	human rights
social activism		

Ellen Ochoa

space shuttle	scholarship	ozone layer
patent	missions specialist	atmosphere
NASA	ultraviolet rays	launch pad

Jaime Escalante

mediocre	discipline	graffiti
Advanced Placement	barrio	calculus
wealthy	showcase	determination

Edward James Olmos

immigrant	diverse	poverty
drama	convicted	narrator
nominated	prejudice	mannerisms
Mafia	activist	volunteerism

Judy Baca

mural
ethnic minorities
prehistoric

rival
tour

Depression
public art

Sandra Cisneros

literature
publication
void

literary agent
observer
unique

fellowship
vintage

Roberto Clemente

foreman
charity
championship

league
relief effort
fielding

career
survivors
Baseball Hall of Fame

Antonia Hernandez

legal
ghetto
counsel
bilingual
contributions

minority group
legal aid
salary
controversial

certificate
legislature
judiciary
unity

Lupe Anguiano

dedicated
bilingual education
welfare
consulting

junior college
employment
diversity

convent
picket lines
model program

Henry B. Gonzalez

Representative
restricted
army intelligence
racial segregation
bribe

fraud
politics
violate
assassin
crisis

senate
translation
filibuster
assassination
saint

Roberto Goizueta

public company	communist	Caribbean
profit	slogan	tradition
soda fountain	international	patriotism

Rita Moreno

seamstress	typecast	reviews
Oscar	Emmy	Tony Award
Grammy Award		

Antonia Novello

surgeon general	surgery	intern
resident	public health	pediatrician
confirmed	alcohol	violence
immunized	prenatal care	

José Feliciano

ghetto	accordion	symphony
mandolin	timbales	bongos
coffeehouse	recording artist	gold record
national anthem		

Ileana Ros-Lehtinen

exile	overthrow	democracy
voting district	election	reelected
opponent		

Answers

CESAR CHAVEZ

Remembering the Facts, p. 5

13. They could not pay the taxes.
14. It is work that requires bending over all day to pick crops.
15. They felt powerless. They didn't speak English, and many were not citizens. The growers were rich and powerful. Workers who angered them might lose their jobs and get sent back to Mexico.
16. He read a lot.
17. The CSO worked to help Mexican Americans better themselves.
18. He used his life savings of $1,200.
19. Five years
20. Marches, boycotts, fasts

Understanding the Story, p. 6

Answers will vary:

21. People on both sides would have been killed. The farmworkers would have been feared and would not have gained the sympathy of the American public.
22. Both fought for civil rights. Both continued the fight at risk of personal danger. Both made impressive gains for oppressed minorities.
23. From his birth he had lived in poverty. His passion was for his work. Money did not matter to him.

Getting the Main Idea, p. 6

His is an inspiring story of how one person can make a huge difference in spite of overwhelming odds.

Applying What You've Learned, p. 6

Students should mention long hours, low pay, poor living conditions, and lack of adequate food.

JOAN BAEZ

Remembering the Facts, pp. 10–11

1. Nonviolence
2. She was dyslexic.
3. Art and music
4. Folk music
5. Newport Jazz Festival in 1959
6. (any two) Civil rights movement; antiwar movement; Cesar Chavez and the Farm Workers
7. She spent more time on her activism than on her music.
8. She was ready to devote more time to her music.

Understanding the Story, p. 11

Answers will vary:
9. Her message was nonviolence. She supported human rights issues in a wide variety of ways.
10. Music and the arts give us hope and beauty even in the worst of times. They refresh our souls and remind us of the good parts of life.

Getting the Main Idea, p. 12

She is a good role model because she has devoted her life to causes and principles she believes in.

Applying What You've Learned, p.12

Encourage students to make a list of ideas that are important to them before they begin their songs or poems.

ELLEN OCHOA

Remembering the Facts, pp. 16–17

1. First female Hispanic astronaut
2. Los Angeles, California
3. Her mother stressed the value of education and hard work.
4. She needed to stay close to home to help her mother with her two younger brothers.
5. Flute
6. She had become interested in being an astronaut and wanted to learn more about flying.
7. Optical processing
8. To study the earth's atmosphere
9. It protects the earth from the sun and its harmful ultraviolet rays.

10. Anyone can succeed if he or she works hard enough in school and on the job.

Understanding the Story, p. 17

Answers will vary:

11. Ochoa's mother practiced what she preached. She taught the children that education was important. They could see how hard she worked to get an education.
12. She feels that her fame has put her in a position to have some influence. She likes to speak to younger children because they are more impressionable. She especially likes to encourage girls to study math and science.

Getting the Main Idea, p. 18

Ellen Ochoa is a good role model because she achieved her success by hard work both in school and on the job.

Applying What You've Learned, p. 18

Students should choose at least seven events to write up as headlines. They should try to make the headlines interesting, not just factual, whenever possible.

JAIME ESCALANTE

Remembering the Facts, pp. 22–23

1. Bolivia
2. Math and science
3. Teachers in Bolivia were so poorly paid that he had to work at three or four jobs.
4. He had to repeat five years of college at an American college.
5. (any three) In the barrio, most students came from poor Hispanic families; gangs; graffiti; trash all over school grounds; most students dropped out; little interest in education
6. To get college credit for a course taken in high school
7. Because so many from one school passed the test; because many students worked one of the questions the same way
8. *Stand and Deliver*
9. Determination + Hard Work + Discipline

Understanding the Story, p. 24

Answers will vary:

10. Other teachers at Garfield were trained by Escalante and had success with his methods. However, a good deal of his success did come from his forceful personality.

11. To be successful and feel good about yourself, it is important to be really good at something.

Getting the Main Idea, p. 24

Escalante is an example of a person who persevered in the face of great odds to do something he loved. He believed that underprivileged students could achieve, and he set out to prove it to them.

Applying What You've Learned, p. 24

Students should choose a job, a celebrity co-host, and a list of ways math is used on that job.

EDWARD JAMES OLMOS

Remembering the Facts, pp. 28–29

1. East Los Angeles
2. In a poor, ethnically diverse neighborhood
3. By becoming a baseball star
4. Eddie James and the Pacific Ocean
5. To overcome his fear of public speaking
6. *Zoot Suit*
7. *Miami Vice*
8. *Stand and Deliver*
9. *American Me*
10. Violence, volunteering

Understanding the Story, pp. 29–30

Answers will vary:
11. Olmos speaks out against violence and for volunteerism. We must speak out against violence and take steps to stop it. Volunteerism is one way to bring a positive influence into the lives of those who see no way out of their situations or who might otherwise succumb to a life of crime or violence.
12. A strong desire to succeed, courage, tenacity, strength of character, clear goals

Getting the Main Idea, p. 30

Olmos is a role model because not only is he a fine actor, but he spends over half his time doing volunteer work, mostly with youth who might be prone to a life of crime and violence.

Applying What You've Learned, p. 30

Explain why nonviolence works best in the long run. Explain that the lives and property of innocent people are being destroyed. Explain that violence will not undo the wrong that was previously done. Ask respected leaders in the community to speak to the people as well.

JUDY BACA

Remembering the Facts, pp. 34–35

1. *The Great Wall of Los Angeles*
2. The history of California
3. Los Angeles
4. She didn't speak English well.
5. She was active in antiwar protests during the Vietnam War.
6. It was a club for youth interested in painting murals.
7. (any three) Prehistoric animals roaming along the tar pits; Cabrillo arriving by ship; Mexicans and Yankees fighting over gold; Chinese workers building the railroad; migrant farm workers working; hungry people lining up for food in the Depression; Japanese Americans being interned during World War II; freedom riders working for civil rights
8. It took place over five summers using 200 multi-ethnic kids. Baca organized the project and raised money for it. She hired other workers and kids to join in.
9. *World Wall: A Vision of the Future Without Fear*
10. She hopes that her work spreads the idea of a world of peace, a world in which everyone is valued. She hopes to teach a spirit of multi-ethnic cooperation.

Understanding the Story, p. 35

Answers will vary:

11. She ended up teaching art to a large number of kids. She also motivated kids from a wide variety of backgrounds to forget their differences and work together.
12. She meant that when people view the artwork, they are exposed to the ideas the artist wants to portray. If you see a painting, you are aware of the idea the artist wants to convey. Similarly if you hear a piece of music, it influences your thinking. You may not even be aware of how it has changed your thinking or your mood at the time.

Getting the Main Idea, p. 36

Judy Baca is a good role model because she is living out her beliefs. From a young age she wanted to work for peace and to solve social problems. Her "public art" has influenced many young people to forget gangs and fighting and work together in peace. She has brought them pride in their history. Now with the *World Wall* she is hoping to spread her ideas around the world.

Applying What You've Learned, p. 36

You may need to preface this activity with a discussion on the history of your town. You could make a list on the board. Then students could make up their own ideas for panels to illustrate some of the events. With a more advanced group, the project could be assigned for independent work.

SANDRA CISNEROS

Remembering the Facts, pp. 40–41

1. Chicago, Illinois
2. Her father would get homesick for Mexico.
3. She was shy. Reading became her escape from her bleak and lonely world.
4. She spent a lot of time observing people.
5. Get married.
6. She became aware of the unique voice she had as a Mexican woman. She accepted herself and went on to tell her story.
7. *The House on Mango Street*
8. She talks about the lives of the people living on Mango Street, a poor Hispanic community in Chicago.
9. The lives of Hispanic women
10. She hopes to tell their story.

Understanding the Story, pp. 41–42

Answers will vary:

11. People who read a lot gain a sense of language and style. They learn how to put thoughts together to tell a story. They gain a rich background of ideas and thoughts.
12. Her background gave her a unique outlook on life. Her habit of staying in the background and observing people gave her a rich storehouse of material for stories. She cares deeply about her subject matter, and that shows in her writing.
13. The experiences you have growing up are an integral part of your being. You can never really leave them behind totally.

Getting the Main Idea, p. 42

Sandra Cisneros is a good role model because she learned to accept herself as she was and to celebrate that unique being in her work. She has dedicated herself to telling the story of her people, her race, and her gender.

Applying What You've Learned, p. 42

Answers will vary.

ROBERTO CLEMENTE

Remembering the Facts, pp. 47–48

1. The Santurce Crabbers
2. Because he had given them his word
3. He felt like an outsider. He faced racial discrimination, different food, and customs. He did not speak English well.
4. Swinging a light bat; a car accident
5. Pittsburgh Pirates
6. He went to Puerto Rico and worked with kids.
7. 3,000
8. To make sure they got to those who needed help
9. (any three) Four National League batting championships; National League's Most Valuable Player 1966, 1971; Twelve Golden Glove awards; Baseball Hall of Fame

Understanding the Story, p. 48

Answers will vary:
10. He was a local boy who had made it big in the States. He had won fame and fortune, but he was never too busy to help someone in need. He devoted much energy to working with the children in Puerto Rico.
11. He felt a responsibility to help humankind. But he did not want praise or recognition for doing what was right. He felt his purpose in life was to help others who needed him.
12. They did not usually feel that comfortable living in the U.S. because of language, customs, and prejudice. They were also probably homesick for their own country.

Getting the Main Idea, p. 48

Roberto Clemente was a National League superstar who also centered his life on helping those less fortunate. He is an excellent role model on how to live your life.

Applying What You've Learned, p. 49

Students should think of a way to motivate their readers to want to get involved in donating to the relief effort.

ANTONIA HERNANDEZ

Remembering the Facts, pp. 54–55

1. MALDEF (Mexican-American Legal Defense Fund)
2. To protect legal rights of Mexican Americans
3. Torreón, Mexico
4. East Los Angeles, California
5. She thought she could help kids more by changing the laws that discriminated against Hispanics.
6. Legal aid lawyer
7. Senate Judiciary Committee
8. To make it easier for students who don't speak English, and to help them maintain their bilingualism and culture
9. When she moved to the East Coast, she met Hispanic Americans from Cuba, Puerto Rico, and Central and South America in addition to those with a Mexican background.
10. She worked with the NAACP on the 1992 Civil Rights Bill.

Understanding the Story, p. 55–56

Answers will vary:

11. Opponents of such programs point to the immense cost involved. They may feel that those who move to the United States need to learn English, not cling to their native tongue. Also, studies have not proven that bilingual education teaches English any better than total immersion in English classes. Those who favor bilingual education say that children have a right to be taught in their native language. They should not have to give up their language for English. They may feel it is discriminatory not to give Spanish equal acceptance with English.
12. All ethnic and racial groups are a part of the history of the United States. All minority groups have faced discrimination and prejudice. Thus, all have the common goal of attaining equality under the law and in practice in daily life.

Getting the Main Idea, p. 56

Hernandez became a lawyer in order to better help her people. She has dedicated her life to helping those in need, whether due to poverty or discrimination.

Applying What You've Learned, p. 56

Students might mention feeling frustrated at not being able to understand. They might be afraid or embarrassed. They might be the object of ridicule. They might start to learn the language by learning the names of objects around them.

Lupe Anguiano

Remembering the Facts, pp. 60–61

1. La Junta, Colorado
2. Migrant farmwork
3. She spoke and wrote only Spanish. She had little formal schooling before she was thirteen.
4. Became a nun
5. To advise him on Mexican-American problems
6. To teach children both in their native language and in English
7. It became remedial classes in English only. Spanish was not taught to these Spanish-speaking children.
8. Set up a grape boycott in Michigan
9. It trained them for jobs. It organized them so some women worked and others cared for the children.
10. Consulting

Understanding the Story, pp. 61–62

Answers will vary:
11. Working to make life better for those in need
12. If they are trained, they can find a decent job. If they have access to good child care, they are free to work and support their own family. This is better for their self-esteem and better for the children to see their parent working to support them.

Getting the Main Idea, p. 62

She is a good role model because she truly cares about the needs of the disadvantaged. She has dedicated her life to helping others. Today she still works to get all Americans working together despite their diversity of race and background.

Applying What You've Learned, p. 62

A good leader must be a person of vision. Vision is needed to see beyond the overwhelming details of a problem and look at the big picture. Vision may help a person see different or unusual ways of looking at a problem. Yet these new and creative solutions to problems must still be practical. If they cannot be put into use, they will never help anyone.

Henry B. Gonzalez

Remembering the Facts, pp. 66–67

1. U.S. Congressman (Representative)
2. San Antonio, Texas
3. He didn't know any English. He was one of just a few Mexican Americans in the class.
4. Law degree
5. (any two) Minority rights; better housing; prevention of a sales tax
6. By taking part in a thirty-six-hour filibuster
7. John F. Kennedy
8. The Affordable Housing Act
9. The savings and loan crisis
10. A reputation for honesty and independence

Understanding the Story, pp. 67–68

Answers will vary:
11. He fights for the rights of minorities. He fights for better housing. He fights hard for the rights of his citizens.
12. Gonzalez has a reputation for honesty. He cannot be bought or bribed. He does not get involved in "dirty politics." He fights for whatever he thinks is right, even if it is not popular.

Getting the Main Idea, p. 68

Gonzalez overcame the racial prejudice of the 1950's by working hard to win respect. He fights hard for his beliefs.

Applying What You've Learned, p. 68

Show students examples of political cartoons to get them started.

Roberto Goizueta

Remembering the Facts, pp. 72–73

1. Havana, Cuba
2. He did not speak English.
3. The country became communist. Castro was taking over businesses and property. Many people were jailed.
4. Chairman and chief executive of Coca-Cola
5. There were older, more experienced people in line. He was from Cuba.
6. Trying to change the formula of Coke®
7. There were two Cokes. The old Coke was called Coca-Cola Classic. The new Coke continued to be sold.
8. Atlanta in 1886

9. The head of the company vowed to provide Coke to soldiers for five cents, no matter where they were. Thus, the government helped build bottling plants overseas.
10. Nearly 50 percent

Understanding the Story, pp. 73–74

Answers will vary:
11. Coke was provided to soldiers overseas. This was a big morale-booster for them. Ads in the States linked Coke with supporting the war effort. When the soldiers came home, they too associated Coke with patriotism.
12. Coke had become a part of the American way of life. It was part of American culture and identity. It ranked right up there with apple pie and motherhood. Changing Coke was like messing up the taste of the most universally enjoyed product in the world.

Getting the Main Idea, p. 74

Goizueta is an example of how anyone can get ahead with hard work and determination.

Applying What You've Learned, p. 74

Students should choose a slogan and create an ad for Coke, using that slogan. The ad should appeal to young people.

RITA MORENO

Remembering the Facts, pp. 78–79

1. She is the only performer who has won all four of entertainment's most important awards.
2. Puerto Rico
3. "Latin spitfire"
4. She became typecast and was only offered this type of role.
5. *The King and I*
6. *West Side Story*
7. *The Electric Company*
8. *The Ritz*
9. *The Muppet Show* or *The Rockford Files*

Understanding the Story, p. 79

Answers will vary:

10. Movie producers at that time were prejudiced against Hispanics and blacks. Since Moreno was a Hispanic woman, they thought of her as a "Latin spitfire." That was the only type of part she was offered. They could not see her in any other type of part because she was Hispanic. Actresses today might meet some of the same type of prejudice. But, according to Edward James Olmos, doors are opening in the movie business for Hispanic Americans.

11. People's heritage is part of who they are. If they reject their heritage, they are rejecting part of themselves. People who embrace their heritage can live a fuller life.

Getting the Main Idea, p. 80

Rita Moreno is a role model because she fought to overcome ethnic stereotypes. She eventually won recognition for her talent.

Applying What You've Learned, p. 80

Students could have Moreno acting in a play or doing a song and dance recital. They could mention her past achievements.

ANTONIA NOVELLO

Remembering the Facts, p. 85

1. First woman, first Hispanic, and first Puerto Rican to be surgeon general
2. Puerto Rico
3. She was born with medical problems and was often ill as a child. Her doctors were her heroes.
4. To protect and improve the health of the American people
5. She worked to ban alcohol ads that target the young. She wanted more alcohol education in schools.
6. She asked tobacco companies to stop ads that appeal to the young.
7. (any three) AIDS; violence; domestic violence; childhood immunizations; prenatal care; better health care for Hispanics

Understanding the Story, p. 86

Answers will vary:

8. She believed that our young people are our future. They cannot speak for themselves; therefore, they need a strong advocate. By preventing young people from using alcohol or tobacco, they will live healthier lives.
9. Alcohol and tobacco use are the major preventable causes of disease. Alcohol use can also lead to other problems such as violence. By curbing the use of these products, Novello could make an impact on the lives of young people.

Getting the Main Idea, p. 86

Novello is a strong, caring person. She has dedicated her life to service for others, especially those who cannot speak up for themselves. She is working hard to make a difference in the lives of the young, the minorities, and the poor in this country.

Applying What You've Learned, p. 86

Some advertising techniques include: using a cartoon character such as "Joe Camel"; making smokers look strong and independent; and portraying smokers or drinkers as having more fun, having more girlfriends or boyfriends, and getting more out of life in general.

JOSÉ FELICIANO

Remembering the Facts, pp. 90–91

1. Puerto Rico
2. Blindness, poverty
3. He tricked the managers into listening to him play.
4. An RCA records man heard him by accident.
5. Latin America (Central and South America)
6. "Light My Fire"
7. Guitar
8. Puerto Rico
9. Hard work
10. "The happy one"

Understanding the Story, pp. 91–92

Answers will vary:

11. Many people felt it was unpatriotic to sing the national anthem in a "Spanish soul" style. They felt it should be done in only one way: the traditional version. In recent years other performers have created controversy with their renditions including Marvin Gaye, Whitney Houston, and Rosanne Barr Arnold.
12. Since he was blind, he concentrated solely on his music with a dedication unusual for a small child, spending most of his free time practicing. If he had had his sight, it is likely that he would not have developed his talent to such a degree so early. However, he would have probably still gone into music.

Getting the Main Idea, p. 92

Feliciano is a good role model because he is a hard worker. He puts everything he's got into what he is doing. He says that hard work is the magic ingredient in success in any field.

Applying What You've Learned, p. 92

Students could mention his awards, his hit records, the date and place of the concert, the cost for tickets, etc.

ILEANA ROS-LEHTINEN

Remembering the Facts, pp. 96–97

1. She was elected to the Florida state legislature.
2. She was elected to the United States Congress.
3. Havana, Cuba
4. Castro came to power.
5. They decided to raise their children as loyal Americans.
6. A teacher, a principal
7. It implied to them that they were not "real" Americans.
8. The Hispanic Americans voted for Ros-Lehtinen; the whites and African Americans voted for Richman.
9. (any one) Bilingual education; seven-day waiting period to buy a handgun; tough sentences for drug dealers
10. She is a strong opponent of Castro.

Understanding the Story, p. 97

Answers will vary:

11. When he took over the country, her family was forced to flee, leaving behind their home and possessions. She feels that he has destroyed her native land.
12. Many middle- and upper-class Cubans came to the United States in 1960. These people have lived here a long time and have built a life for themselves here. They would be more likely to stay here. Other Cubans came to the United States in the 1980's. More are coming now. These people have weaker ties to the United States and would be more likely than earlier arrivals to return to Cuba.

Getting the Main Idea, p. 98

She is a good role model because she has worked hard to achieve her goals. She is working hard for all the people of her congressional district.

Applying What You've Learned, p. 98

You could mention that Cuban Americans, like other immigrants to this country, are real Americans. All citizens should have equal rights, including the right to run for office. You could mention America as a great melting pot of many cultures and nationalities . . .

Additional Activities

Cesar Chavez

1. Read John Steinbeck's book *The Grapes of Wrath*. This is a vivid account of the life of migrant workers in the 1930's in California.

2. Mahatma Gandhi was Chavez's hero. Read more about Gandhi's philosophy.

3. Read more about the Great Depression of the 1930's. Why did so many small farmers lose their farms at this time, as Chavez's parents did?

4. Read about Saul Alinsky, a Chicago activist who founded the Community Service Organization.

Joan Baez

1. Read more about the 1960's civil rights movement in the United States.

2. Find out more about the antiwar movement in the 1960's.

3. Obtain one of Baez's early folk music recordings. Listen to it in class.

4. Read Baez's autobiography *And a Voice to Sing With*.

5. Listen to some of Baez's later recordings. What themes do you hear running through her music?

Ellen Ochoa

1. Franklin Chang-Diaz was the first male Hispanic astronaut. Find out more about his life.

2. Read more about the *Discovery* space shuttle.

3. Find out more about the ozone layer. Why are scientists concerned about the fact that it is thinning? What can be done to save the ozone layer?

Jaime Escalante

1. Watch the movie *Stand and Deliver*, starring Edward James Olmos as Jaime Escalante.

2. Watch the special "Math . . . Who Needs It?" starring Jaime Escalante and Bill Cosby, or read the paperback version of this PBS special.

3. *Futures* is a series of shows distributed by PBS for in-classroom viewing by students in grades six to twelve. Each show features a celebrity guest who, together with Escalante, shows how math is used in a selected occupation. See if your school's math department has copies of these shows. For information on ordering the series call PBS Video, Alexandria, VA, at 1–800–344–3337.

4. Find out what types of Advanced Placement courses are available in your local high school. How many students pass the AP test for college credit in calculus? in other subjects?

Edward James Olmos

1. View one of Edward James Olmos's movies:

   Zoot Suit
   The Ballad of Gregorio Cortez
   Stand and Deliver
   Wolfen
   Blade Runner
   Triumph of the Spirit
   Talent for the Game
   American Me

2. Read more about the Los Angeles riots of 1992 and the Rodney King incident.

3. Discuss the issue of increasing violence in America. What do you think can be done about it in your community?

Judy Baca

1. Find out more about the protest movements during the Vietnam War.

2. In Mexico, mural painting is an old tradition. Find out more about one of these famous Mexican mural painters: Diego Rivera, David Alfaro Siqueiros, or José Clemente Orozco.

Sandra Cisneros

1. Read the book *The House on Mango Street.* (The book is composed of vignettes of one to three pages each. This makes it ideal for reading aloud in small segments to students.)

2. Read to the class selections from Cisneros's other books:

   Woman Hollering Creek and Other Stories (1992)
   My Wicked, Wicked Ways (1987)
   Loose Woman (1994)

Roberto Clemente

1. Read and report on another Hispanic-American baseball player of your choice. Some examples are: Luis Aparicio, Rod Carew, Orlando Cepeda, Martin Dihigo, Tony Fernandez, Lefty Gomez, Keith Hernandez, Al Lopez, Juan Marichal, José Mendez, Orestes Minoso, Tony Oliva, Alejandro Oms, Luis Tiant, Fernando Valenzuela, Pedro Guerroro, Rafael Santana, George Bell, Joaquin Andujar, Alfredo Griffin, Julio Franco, Ozzie Virgil, Felipe Alou, Mario Soto, and many, many more.

2. Find Puerto Rico on a map. Look up some information about this island that belongs to the United States.

3. Read about the earthquake in Nicaragua in 1972.

4. Find out more about the Pittsburgh Pirates in the 1950's and 1960's.

5. Read about Branch Rickey, manager of the Pirates for part of Clemente's career. Branch Rickey was also the man who signed Jackie Robinson, the first African American in pro ball.

6. Read about the old Negro League baseball teams.

7. Find out how the Dodgers lost Clemente to the Pirates.

Antonia Hernandez

1. Read more about the story of MALDEF, the Mexican-American Legal Defense Fund.

2. Find out more about the Civil Rights Law of 1992.

3. Have a classroom debate about bilingual education, or have students write a paragraph giving their opinion on a topic such as: Should education for Spanish-speaking children be bilingual or traditional? (Bilingual education tends to be an emotional issue. Some people resent the expense of providing special classes for Spanish-speaking children. They feel that it is the immigrant's duty to learn the language of their adopted country. Others feel the Spanish-speaking children should be given instruction in both languages, enabling them to become bilingual.)

4. In 1994 a bill (H.R. 739) went before Congress that would make English the official language of the United States. This would mean that all business of the federal government would be conducted in English. It would also repeal laws that require bilingual education and multilingual ballots. Discuss the pros and cons of this bill.

5. As of 1994, eighteen states had made English their official language. This relieves them of the responsibility of providing separate services for Spanish-speaking people. Such a measure was passed in 1980 in Dade County, Florida, where half the people speak Spanish at home. However, in May 1993, this law was overturned. At present Dade County is multilingual. Discuss the problems that having a multilingual county would cause.

6. One poll indicated that 98 percent of Hispanic parents thought it was important for their children to read and write English "per-fectly." Discuss how this goal might be best achieved.

7. In 1990 one school district in Oakland, California, was required by state law to offer students instruction in Spanish, Lao, Khmer, Tigrinya (an Ethiopian language), Cantonese, and Vietnamese. What problems would this create for the school district?

Lupe Anguiano

1. Read more about Anguiano's work with Cesar Chavez organizing the grape boycott in Michigan.

2. Find out more about Aid to Families with Dependent Children (AFDC).

Henry B. Gonzalez

1. Read more about the assassination of President John F. Kennedy and the conspiracy theory favored by Gonzalez.

2. Read more about the savings and loan scandal.

3. Gonzalez called for the impeachment of President Ronald Reagan for the U.S. invasion of Grenada and again for the Iran Contra affair. Read more about these events.

4. In 1991 Gonzalez called for the impeachment of President George Bush for going to war with Iraq over the fate of Kuwait without seeking a formal declaration of war from Congress. Read more about this war called "Desert Storm."

Roberto Goizueta

1. The story of the Coca-Cola Company makes interesting reading. Find out more about the history of Coke.

2. The media were almost universally against the introduction of new Coke. Write a short newspaper article telling why the Coke formula should not be changed. Write a catchy headline to go with the story.

3. Read more about Fidel Castro and his rise to power in Cuba.

4. Look at the New York Stock Exchange quotes in the newspaper. What is the price of a share of Coke stock?

5. Find out what soft drinks are marketed by Coca-Cola today.

Rita Moreno

1. Obtain a copy of one of Rita Moreno's movies. *The King and I* or *West Side Story* would be good choices.

2. Obtain a copy of Rita Moreno's Grammy-winning album of songs from the TV show *The Electric Company*.

Antonia Novello

1. Report on one of the following problems: alcohol use among teens; teen smoking; AIDS among teens; teens and violent crimes; teen pregnancy.

2. Discuss the effects of advertising on behavior. What ads have you seen for alcohol or tobacco that make you want to try the product advertised? Why?

3. Discuss immunizations that are required for a child to attend public school. What are these immunizations (polio, diphtheria, tetanus and whooping cough, measles)? Why do many children not receive these immunizations?

José Feliciano

1. Listen to one of Feliciano's albums. Discuss his style. He has recorded forty-eight albums. Some of the biggest sellers are:

   Feliciano, 1968
   Encore!, 1971
   Fireworks, 1974
   Escenas de Amor, 1982
   A Bag Full of Soul, 1983
   Romance in the Night, 1983
   Portrait, 1985
   Latin Street '92, 1992

2. Find Feliciano's birthplace, Lares, Puerto Rico, on a map. Read more about that part of Puerto Rico.

3. Read about "Spanish Harlem," a Hispanic ghetto in New York City.

Ileana Ros-Lehtinen

1. Read more about Fidel Castro and his rise to power in Cuba. Find out why so many middle- and upper-class Cubans fled to the United States in 1960.

2. Read about the Bay of Pigs invasion.

3. Find out more about the city of Miami and its Cuban-American population.

References

General References

Catalano, Julie. *The Mexican Americans.* New York: Chelsea House Publishers, 1988.

Dwyer, Christopher. *The Dominican Americans.* New York: Chelsea House Publishers, 1991.

Gernand, Renee. *The Cuban Americans.* New York: Chelsea House Publishers, 1988.

Grenquist, Barbara. *Cubans.* New York: Franklin Watts, 1991.

Kanellos, Nicholas, ed. *Hispanic-American Almanac: A Reference Work on Hispanics in the United States.* Detroit: Gale Research, 1993.

Katz, William Loren. *Minorities Today.* Austin, Texas: Raintree Steck-Vaughn, 1993.

Larsen, Ronald J. *The Puerto Ricans in America.* Minneapolis: Lerner Publications, 1974.

Who's Who Among Hispanic Americans? Detroit: Gale Research, 1991.

Lupe Anguiano

Newlon, Clarke. *Famous Mexican Americans.* New York: Dodd, Mead, 1972, p. 153+.

Telgen, Diane, and Kamp, Jim, eds. *Notable Hispanic-American Women.* Detroit: Gale Research, 1993, pp. 22–24.

Judy Baca

"Judy Baca." *Life*, December 1980, pp. 87–90.

Lippard, Lucy R. *Mixed Blessings: New Art in a Multicultural America.* New York: Pantheon Books, 1990, pp. 170–171.

Telgen, Diane, and Kamp, Jim, eds. *Notable Hispanic-American Women.* Detroit: Gale Research, 1993, pp. 35–38.

Joan Baez

Baez, Joan. *And a Voice to Sing With: A Memoir.* New York: Summit Books, 1987.

Foy, William. "Times a-Changing for Baez: Folk Singer Puts New Emphasis on Music." (Eau Clair, WI) *Leader Telegram*, January 27, 1994.

The Marshall Cavendish Illustrated History of Popular Music, Vol. 6. New York: Marshall Cavendish Corp., 1989, pp. 670–673.

Telgen, Diane, and Kamp, Jim, eds. *Notable Hispanic-American Women.* Detroit: Gale Research, 1993, pp. 42–45.

Cesar Chavez

Current Biography Yearbook. New York: H.W. Wilson Co., 1969, pp. 86–89.

Current Biography Yearbook. New York: H.W. Wilson Co., 1993, Obituaries.

"His Harvest Was Dignity." *People*, May 10, 1993.

Roberts, Naurice. *Cesar Chavez and La Causa.* Chicago: Children's Press, 1986.

Taylor, Ronald B. *Chavez and the Farm Workers.* Boston: Beacon Press, 1975.

Sandra Cisneros

Cisneros, Sandra. *The House on Mango Street*. New York: Random House, 1989. (First published by Arte Publico Press in 1984.)

———— . "Only Daughter." *Glamour*. Vol. 88, No. 11, November, 1990, pp. 256–257.

Sagel, Jim. "Sandra Cisneros." *Publisher's Weekly*, Vol. 238, Issue 15, March 29, 1991, pp. 74–75.

Telgen, Diane, and Kamp, Jim, eds. *Notable Hispanic-American Women*. Detroit: Gale Research, 1993, pp. 99–101.

Roberto Clemente

Gutelle, Andrew. *Baseball's Best: 5 True Stories*. New York: Random House, 1990.

United Press International. *Clemente*. New York: Grosset & Dunlap, 1973.

Waggenheim, Kal. *Clemente*. New York: Praeger Publications, 1973.

Jaime Escalante

Mathews, Jay. "Escalante Still Stands and Delivers." *Time*, July 20, 1992.

———— . *Escalante: The Best Teacher in America*. New York: Holt, 1988.

"Teacher Advises Positive Attitude." *Clarion Ledger* (Jackson, MS), October 18, 1994.

Warner Brothers. *Stand and Deliver* (film). 1988.

José Feliciano

Clifford, Mike, ed. *The Harmony Illustrated History of Rock*. New York: Harmony Books, 1986, p. 80.

Pareles, Jon, and Romanowski, Patricia, eds. *The Rolling Stone Encyclopedia of Rock and Roll*. New York: Rolling Stone Press, 1983, pp. 184–187.

Rostova, Carolina Ruiz. "A Latin Legend in the Jazz World." *Stamford* (CT) *Advocate*, January 7, 1994.

Roberto Goizueta

Grossman, Laurie M. "Coke's Move to Retain Goizueta Spotlights a Succession Problem." *Wall Street Journal*, May 13, 1994.

Huey, John. "The World's Best Brand." *Fortune*, May 31, 1993.

Ingham, John N., and Feldman, Lynne B., eds. *Contemporary American Business Leaders: A Biographical Dictionary.* Westport, CT: Greenwood Press, 1990, pp. 166–176.

Henry B. Gonzalez

Current Biography Yearbook. New York: H.W. Wilson Co., 1993, pp. 214–217.

Newlon, Clarke. *Famous Mexican Americans.* New York: Dodd, Mead, 1972.

Antonia Hernandez

Grolier, Ingrid. "Law in the Family." *Parents*, March 1985, pp. 96–100; 170–174.

Gross, Liza. "Antonia Hernandez: MALDEF's Legal Eagle." *Hispanic*, December 1990, pp. 16–18.

"Interview: Antonia Hernandez." *Dallas* (TX) *Texas Morning News,* 1992.

Telgen, Diane, and Kamp, Jim, eds. *Notable Hispanic-American Women.* Detroit: Gale Research, 1993, pp. 196–198.

Rita Moreno

Current Biography Yearbook. New York: H.W. Wilson Co., 1985, pp. 299–302.

Mastrolanni, Tony. "The Versatile Rita Moreno Taking the Stage." *Ohio Beacon Journal*, November 3, 1991.

Telgen, Diane, and Kamp, Jim, eds. *Notable Hispanic-American Women.* Detroit: Gale Research, 1993, pp. 286–290.

Antonia Novello

Cohen, Charles E. "Butt Out, Guido Sarcucci!" *People,* 34: 109ff., December 16, 1990.

Current Biography Yearbook. New York: H.W. Wilson Co., 1992, pp. 422–426.

Novello, Antonia. "Health Priorities for the Nineties." Speech at the Town Hall of California, Los Angeles, CA, April 21, 1992. *Vital Speeches of the Day,* Vol. 58, Issue 21, Aug. 15, 1992, pp. 666–672.

———. "Your Parents, Your Community: Without Caring There Is No Hope." Speech at Georgetown University School of Medicine Commencement Activities, Washington, DC, May 29, 1993. *Vital Speeches of the Day,* Vol. 59, Issue 19, July 15, 1993, pp. 588–592.

Ellen Ochoa

"Ellen Ochoa." *Hispanic*, May 1990, pp. 18–19.

"La Mesa Astronaut Set to Soar." *San Diego Union*, April 5, 1993.

Telgen, Diane, and Kamp, Jim, eds. *Notable Hispanic-American Women.* Detroit: Gale Research, 1993, pp. 296–299.

Edward James Olmos

Current Biography Yearbook. New York: H.W. Wilson Co., 1992, pp. 426–430.

Garcia, Guy D. "Burning With Passion." *Time*, July 13, 1988.

Szegedy-Maszak, Marianne. "The Activist Actor." *USA Weekend*, May 20–22, 1994.

Ileana Ros-Lehtinen

Black, Chris. "Exile Politics Shaped Passions of New Florida Congresswoman." *Boston Globe*, August 31, 1989.

"Ileana Ros-Lehtinen." *Hispanic*, October 1990, pp. 26–27.

Telgen, Diane, and Kamp, Jim, eds. *Notable Hispanic-American Women.* Detroit: Gale Research, 1991, pp. 356–358.